W0115319

11·7·14

Dave,

Thanks for showing me what leader evolution looks like. I truly value our relationship.

Alan

Leader Evolution

Leader Evolution

From Technical Expertise to Strategic Leadership

Alan Patterson

BEP BUSINESS EXPERT PRESS

Leader Evolution: From Technical Expertise to Strategic Leadership
Copyright © Business Expert Press, LLC, 2015.
All rights reserved. No part of this publication may be reproduced, stored in a retrieval system, or transmitted in any form or by any means—electronic, mechanical, photocopy, recording, or any other except for brief quotations, not to exceed 400 words, without the prior permission of the publisher.

First published in 2015 by
Business Expert Press, LLC
222 East 46th Street, New York, NY 10017
www.businessexpertpress.com

ISBN-13: 978-1-60649-910-8 (paperback)
ISBN-13: 978-1-60649-911-5 (e-book)

Business Expert Press Human Resource Management and Organizational Behavior Collection

Collection ISSN: 1946-5637 (print)
Collection ISSN: 1946-5645 (electronic)

Cover and interior design by Exeter Premedia Services Private Ltd., Chennai, India

First edition: 2015

10 9 8 7 6 5 4 3 2 1

Printed in the United States of America.

In memory of Ronna Alintuck, who told me that the only difference between people who write books and people who don't write books is that they do it.

Abstract

Most individuals who move into leadership positions experience the modern day version of trial by ordeal. It's sink or swim. To reduce the learning curve and create a more effective process, *Leader Evolution* describes a road map for leadership development, a series of four stages that expand personal competence as well as create a broader impact on the organization or business. Each stage requires unique changes in thinking, perspective taking, and behavior, both those needed to acquire as well as those needed to jettison. The book is a pragmatic approach for self-motived individuals to take control of their professional development by giving them the concepts, tools, techniques, and assignments to develop their leadership effectiveness where it counts the most—on the job.

In addition to new and existing managers, the book is ideally suited for technical professionals and leaders in technical organizations looking to develop critical leadership behaviors distinct from technical expertise. These include individuals who are moving on a technical rather than managerial track. The broad application of concepts and techniques also makes this book appealing to organizations developing their leaders as part of broad change initiatives. While the concepts and principles are directed toward the individual for on-the-job application, the book serves as an organizational and leadership development resource for Executive MBA programs as well as a blueprint for in-house leadership development programs.

Keywords

adaptability, alignment, analytical thinking, authentic leadership, change management, coaching, competency-based, credibility, culture, emotional intelligence, high performance organization, leadership, leadership development, leadership style, leadership training, management, mentor, metacognition, motivation, partnership, professional development, strategic, strategy, strategic thinking, succession planning, talent development, talent management, teamwork, technical leadership, training

Contents

Preface

The Challenges of Leadership Development

Somewhere in a courtroom in Europe in the mid-eleventh century a judge orders the bandages removed from the hand of an accused criminal. Three days earlier, the suspect was forced to pull an iron ring out of a cauldron of boiling water. If the hand is unharmed, he is innocent; if not, he is guilty, not to mention most likely suffering from third-degree burns. At another time in another courtroom the suspect in question is bound and thrown into a pool of water. If he sinks, he's innocent; if he floats, he's rewarded with a free, darkened cell with form-fitting chains and shackles for the rest of his life. Such practices were common in the Dark Ages: trial by ordeal; justice, medieval style.[1] Some 10 centuries later, however, there are people inside today's organizations who might describe their passage from individual contributor and expert roles into leadership positions as a modern-day trial by ordeal, often characterized as baptism by fire or drinking from a fire hose.

This is not to say that all individuals moving into or currently working in leadership positions were left to sink or swim on their own. There are many organizations that have top-flight programs and proven track records of increasing their leadership capacity and subsequently their profitability.[2] They appreciate the win–win outcomes for the individual and the organization achieved by developing leadership at all levels of the organization. In 2013, the Hay Group identified the top 20 companies in this area. At the top of the list were Procter & Gamble, Microsoft, General Electric, Coca-Cola, and Unilever.[3] They also reported that 73 percent of the top 20 offered broad-based talent development opportunities to every employee. These companies and others like them see leadership development as an investment, not an expense. What one is likely to see throughout these organizations are:

- Employees who are willing and open to continuous learning, and who take an active role in their professional development
- A developmental road map that clearly identifies the skills, competencies, and behaviors needed to succeed as a leader
- A cadre of managers that takes leadership seriously, particularly when it comes to the coaching and teaching role
- A talent development culture, meaning that there is both an underlying belief that people make the difference and an appropriate infrastructure for developing talent that supports this belief throughout the organization

Over the broader landscape, however, there are marked differences in how leaders are developed and a somewhat less-than-certain view of a planned, methodical road map for success. Some individuals are fortunate to have at least key pieces of the leadership development process. For example, maybe you have a good manager as a teacher and coach and a clearly defined succession plan with developmental assignments and opportunities that await you. Perhaps, you have taken several courses that your organization offers, like a class on communication and feedback skills or a three-day training workshop on the secrets to successful middle management. Maybe, you've had an opportunity to take a college course, or enroll in an MBA program with financial assistance from your organization. Perhaps, you've had a 360 feedback assessment, or a chance to lead a highly visible cross-functional project. Or, maybe, you are one of the less fortunate who were bound and tossed into the deep end of the organizational pool, to sink or swim on your own, left to figure things out, both the basics and subtleties of leadership for yourself.

Who Is Responsible for Your Development as a Leader?

In today's constantly changing, resource-constrained world, leadership development can be a hit or miss process. We acknowledge those top-flight, investment-based professional development organizations. Yet, there are others who see leadership development as an expense. When dollars are scarce, professional development is often a target, and as the definition states, "the aim of an attack."

As a new or prospective leader, a current leader, or a technical professional looking to broaden your career, take notice. This wide range of approaches raises a very important question. *Who is responsible for your development as a leader?* That would be you. The question of who owns *your* professional development and developing *your* leadership chops is best answered by the person you see in the mirror.

The purpose of this book is to give you as a self-motivated professional a developmental road map for how to move from a base of expertise to a position of strategic leadership. The concept of position is not just a reference to a specific job in the organizational hierarchy. It also refers to a role of expanded influence that you develop through an evolutionary process. This book is not about positions or titles. It is about how stepping up and expanding your personal capability can have a broader, positive impact on organizational capability and subsequent long-term success, creating classic win–win outcomes. It is a guide and a map of not only the skills and behaviors needed for effective leadership, but also the critical shifts needed in thinking and perspective-taking. It is intended to make you think about how you think. Ultimately, it means that there must be changes in where and how you spend your time that define success—both to you and your organization—as you progress in your career.

To this end, I have created this book with three audiences in mind. Each shares a similar process for strategic leadership development but varies based on unique combinations of both technical skills and critical behaviors required in a particular stage or role:

1. *New leaders with one to two years of experience, looking to learn the ropes*
   The key for a new leader is to get grounded in leadership principles and key skill development areas such as building trust, credibility, communication, influence, motivation, and managing relationships. Since many new leaders come from the ranks of individual contributors, it is also important to understand where and how you spend your time, meaning how to let go of certain hands-on activities and how to increase your capability of executing through others.

2. *Current leaders with increased responsibilities for running the organization or business*

At a certain point in the development of expanded leadership capability, your value is derived by the extent to which you build and expand organizational capacity. Often the business describes its needs as "operating at a higher level." What this means is more focus on the conditions for successful execution, issues such as organizational alignment, talent development, and effective change leadership, far beyond the basics of managing performance. At another key stage in the evolution of your leadership capability, there are broader requirements—to see the bigger picture, to think strategically, and to study how the business creates value and derives profit, all of which comprise "business savvy."

3. *Technical experts moving into strategic roles in organizations where technical knowledge and expertise are core to the business.*

As a point of clarification, throughout this book the terms *expert* and *expertise* are used broadly to refer to the content-related or knowledge-based component of any job or role. Certain jobs such as engineering, information technology, the sciences, and research and development are highly technical in nature. For these professions and organizations, the terms *expert* and *expertise* have specific meaning. Other jobs, however, have knowledge-based components where these terms are used more generally.

In technical organizations, meaning those businesses or functional organizations where technical expertise is the core, there are often individuals who are more interested in a career based on increased technical experience and application as opposed to entering the management ranks. Depending on the size and type of organization, this choice is facilitated either through a dual career track with technical and managerial options, or a less-formal, personal arrangement for career development. In either scenario, the appeal to you as a member of this audience is that your strategic value over time is a unique combination of technical expertise, credibility, and business acumen, a type of "technical savvy" that is discussed in Chapter 6.

The Mentoré Leadership Model

The developmental road map used in this work is based on a set of competencies known as the Mentoré Leadership Model, a framework I created for use with my clients. It consists of the appropriate skill sets needed in moving from a base of expertise to strategic leadership positions. The map consists of four broad regions or stages of development. Each stage represents a unique mindset and perspective as well as skills, competencies, and behaviors. Holistically, these stages represent how leaders evolve from a base of personal competence to higher-level requirements needed for increased organizational capacity and ongoing business success. The development of leadership capability as an evolutionary and competency-based process is similar across businesses and organizations. However, what's different is how organizations carve out leadership roles and responsibilities. This means that the importance, intensity, and timing of leadership-related behaviors and thought processes will vary by position, function, organization, or business. Specifically, what leadership "looks like" in any given position is important to determine, and we address this straightaway in the first chapter.

The Mentoré model and road map are also the organizing principles for the book:

- Chapter 1 describes the context for leadership. It begins with a brief history of leadership theory, the rise of competency research, and the implications for a behavioral approach to professional development. There is also an overview of the Mentoré model, which is used as an integrative mechanism throughout the book to describe the process of evolution across stages and corresponding sets of competencies.
- Chapter 2 is a discussion of the first stage of leadership development, building a base of expertise. Expertise as mastery, a combination of skills and applied knowledge, is built upon a unique set of attributes that evolve throughout the leadership development process.

- Chapter 3 is a description of the second leadership stage, credibility. Credibility is the foundation for building and managing relationships. Broadly speaking, this stage describes the thought processes and behaviors popularized by Daniel Goldman as emotional intelligence.[4]

Chapters 2 and 3 are particularly relevant to the first time leader because they describe the importance of building a track record of success and adding value to others in the organization as foundational elements for effective leadership. It is also important for those individuals in highly technical roles to consider because of the important role credibility plays in achieving recognition and status as a subject matter expert.

- Chapter 4 describes alignment and execution, the stage in a leader's development where the ability to impact the organization by achieving results through others trumps personal expertise. Many of the traditional leadership skills related to elevating team performance are critical at this stage. Also discussed are thinking in terms of systems, creating and maintaining organizational alignment, leading change, developing talent, and serving as a role model to others.
- Chapter 5 describes what it means to be strategic and how life at this stage of development is critical for the sustainability of the enterprise. The ability to see the big picture and translate the future into present terms is an essential element in strategic leadership. Being strategic also necessitates understanding the business, much broader than simply the experience gained from your own particular functional specialty.

Chapters 4 and 5 are particularly critical for existing managers and those professionals moving further along the technical track, beyond the stage of personal credibility and a track record of personal success. As either a people manager or higher-level technical professional, you have more responsibility for leading the organization and impacting at least your part of the business. These chapters address what are the differences in mindset, perspective, and focus as well as behavior. Collectively, these significantly change where and how you spend your time.

- Chapter 6 is the unique journey for technical professionals moving into strategic technical leadership positions, specifically the need to defy the gravitational pull of hands-on, knowledge-based expertise at every point along the way.
- The final chapter summarizes the important concepts and poses the challenge for how you plan to move forward into strategic leadership roles.

This book is not about identifying your next job or guaranteeing how to become a successful executive. It's about how you move from a base of knowledge and hands-on experience to strategic leader-

Who is responsible for your development as a leader? That would be you.

ship positions, meaning how you have a positive impact on the business, and a meaningful career for yourself. Your path may go the way of a traditional manager of people, or it may be as a high-level technical professional. However, as both focus on the business, both are strategic and important.

By reading and thinking through the concepts in *Leader Evolution*, the goal is to help you gain deeper insight into:

1. The use of a developmental road map to chart your future leadership development
2. What leadership looks like from a behavioral perspective
3. Why and when you need to change focus, thought process, and perspective as you move through different stages
4. Why thinking about thinking becomes increasingly more important as a component of strategic leadership and how it changes where and how you spend your time throughout the evolutionary process

If there are no questions, let's get started.

Acknowledgments

For me, writing this book was like learning to fly an airplane. I have done my fair share of flying as a passenger throughout my professional career. I have seen thousands of planes, observed hundreds of pilots, and offered a multitude of opinions on what differentiates a superior versus average landing and takeoff. But I have never sat in the pilot's seat and flown the plane, until now.

I did not fly solo. Several people were by my side throughout the trip. While some pushed and several challenged me, all supported me at every step. My brother, Dr. Larry Patterson, was both my inspiration and my Jiminy Cricket, asking, telling, and often strongly recommending for me to stay the course. As a former flight school instructor, he knows what it takes to become a pilot. Dr. Robert Hewes of Camden Consulting, in Boston, taught me the discipline of setting goals and writing daily, but more importantly, he has shown me what it means to be a colleague and friend. Bob and I have spent countless hours batting around concepts and ideas about effective leadership development. Bob is an anchor, and if there is one thing a divergent thinker needs, it is an anchor.

Another colleague, Dr. Matt Doll of Fond du Lac, Wisconsin, is a brilliant psychologist and community activist, not to mention a creative and strategic thinker. Matt indulged me in more tangential thinking than any one person deserves, and with his help we destroyed many, if not all of the boxes from which we are told to think out of. Marian Sheridan is much more than a friend and professional colleague. Throughout every discussion that we have had either over meals, holidays, coffee, or snow shoeing, she offered nothing less than the gifts of engagement and encouragement. Oh yes, Marian challenged me as well.

Meeting Rob Zwettler of Business Express Press has proven to be more than just a serendipitous encounter as students in a photography class last summer. Through Rob's guidance and that of his capable collection editors, I am able to finally convert thinking about writing into writing about thinking. With Destiny Hadley's steady guidance as production manager at Business Expert Press and the editing team at Exeter, the details for this book were nailed down. They are the yin to my yang, and without them, I could never have completed this project.

And most of all, to Sheli for your continuous support, thank you barely fills a thimble of overflowing gratitude and joy. You always open windows when doors are shut. This is your gift, and I am grateful.

CHAPTER 1

A Context for Leadership Development

What is leadership? Often leadership is equated with people skills or described as "soft skills." Sometimes, leadership is distinguished from management, where experts like John Kotter link leadership with change and management with predictability and order.[1] For our purpose, *leadership is the ability to influence the ways people think and feel to the point that they take decisive and responsible action.* Leadership is selling ideas, motivating teams, gaining commitment, modeling behavior, engaging in dialogue, aligning organizations, and getting results. It's a skill set that runs the gamut from easy to train to downright difficult to develop. Some people acquire these naturally, but most acquire them through practice and application. Some learn leadership through role models and mentors if they're lucky, others through training programs, and most by osmosis. The point is that we can define leadership as a set of behaviors, and as behaviors, new and existing leaders can see it, learn it, and get better at it.

A Brief History of Leadership Theory

Leadership was not always considered as behaviors related to influence. For more than two centuries, people have studied leadership to understand its origin, characteristics, and effectiveness.[2] Beginning in the mid-19th century, the prevailing leadership concept was that of the "great man," a generalized yet nonscientific acceptance that, as the name implies, only certain people were capable of leadership. Writer and historian Thomas Carlyle popularized this concept in his book *On Heroes, Hero Worship, and the Heroic in History*.[3] In the 1930s and 1940s, the American psychologist Gordon Allport described certain personality characteristics that are indicative of successful leaders.[4] Allport claimed that leaders are born with certain traits and exhibit them in certain combinations that make them successful. As the field of psychometrics grew from the 1930s to 1950s, however, additional scientific researchers had difficulty showing consistent results when using traits to define leadership success.[5]

Behavior Theory

The failure to show reliable and consistent correlations between traits and leadership gave rise to new concepts. Researchers began looking at behavior rather than trait to measure leadership effectiveness. Since behaviors are observable, it makes them much easier to study and understand. One understands leadership by how someone *acts*, not simply by the traits they may or may not possess.[6]

Most notably in this era were two key university studies conducted at Ohio State University and the University of Michigan.[7] The Ohio State studies used a series of statements to measure leadership on nine behavioral dimensions. The two most highly correlated sets of behaviors were characterized as "consideration" or people-related issues, and "initiating structure" or task-related issues. Dr. Rensis Likert at the University of Michigan undertook a similar approach to the study of leadership. Likert's research identified three critical types of leadership behavior:

- Task–oriented behavior such as planning, organizing, and monitoring
- Relationship–oriented behavior such as supporting, motivating, and rewarding
- Participative leadership such as facilitating rather than directing the team[8]

Contingency Theory: One Size Does Not Fit All

By the mid-20th century, a new interest in understanding leadership behavior emerged. Rather than focus on the *either–or* characteristics of task-related and relationship-related behaviors, R.R. Blake and J.S. Mouton used both sets to determine leadership effectiveness based on situational requirements. This approach was known as the managerial grid, and it provided a conceptual framework for leadership styles.[9] Styles are collections of behaviors dependent on the situation and needs of people involved. Hersey and Blanchard popularized this concept as "situational leadership."[10]

Contingency theory continues to impact our modern-day perspective on leadership effectiveness in two ways:

1. Leadership requires both managing tasks and managing people.
2. There is no one "correct" style of leadership. Instead, the "correctness" depends on the leader's ability to scope out the situation and use the behaviors suited to the individuals involved.

Transformational Leadership Theory

In the 1970s and 1980s, a different leadership concept known as transformational leadership came to light from researchers such as Bass[11] and Burns.[12] In transformational leadership, the leader's role is to create and sell a compelling vision that (a) motivates people to operate at a higher level and (b) creates a greater sense of purpose. Transformational leaders are concerned less with task-specific needs and more with building trust, selling ideas, and gaining commitment. The vision is the transformative mechanism, the "big picture" that so often is missing in the day-to-day frenzy of modern organizations. In Chapter 5, we will discuss why this capability is so important.

The Rationale for a Behavioral Approach to Leadership Development

Leadership in today's world is a mix of the conceptual and pragmatic, scientific and artistic, and predictive and situational. Developing leaders require a disciplined, practical approach based on the acquisition and demonstration of critical behaviors, skills sets, and competencies. Competencies are the characteristics that define outstanding performance. One of the pioneers in the field of competency research is David McClelland.[13] McClelland also spawned a generation of researchers that include experts such as Richard Boyatzis,[14] Lyle Spencer,[15] and Daniel Goleman.[16]

There are two questions to consider in using a behavioral approach to leadership development:

1. What is the level of effort needed to acquire these behaviors?
2. To what extent are there identifiable stages that uniquely characterize leadership behavior, thought processes, and perspectives at certain points in your career?

What Is the Level of Effort Needed to Acquire Leadership Behaviors?

There are certain assumptions that one makes when adopting a behavioral approach to leadership development. First, focusing on behavior is a way to dissect what people do from deeper, more personality-based characteristics such as traits or aptitudes. While the dissection is possible, it does not negate the possibility that some of the behaviors are linked to something deeper inside one's personality. This raises the question of trainability: How much effort is needed to acquire a specific behavior?

Using a pyramid as a concept, consider the characteristics about how people differ. At the top of the pyramid are knowledge and skills. Below these are aptitudes, which are more innate and often described as "natural abilities." Moving down the pyramid are traits or personality characteristics, values and beliefs, and motives. The characteristics at the top are more observable and easier to train. At the bottom are more innate characteristics that are closely associated with who we are, what we believe, and what drives us. These are less observable and take more time to develop.

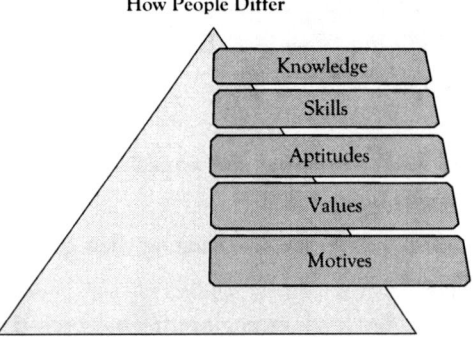

How People Differ

There are, however, behavioral links between those characteristics at the top and at the bottom. For example, it may be difficult to change someone's basic motivation for achievement at a "gut level," but it is possible to teach and learn the behaviors for *how to* set goals and achieve results. This suggests that rather than trying to "teach" basic motives, values, or traits, it is better to identify and develop the behaviors that are associated with these characteristics.

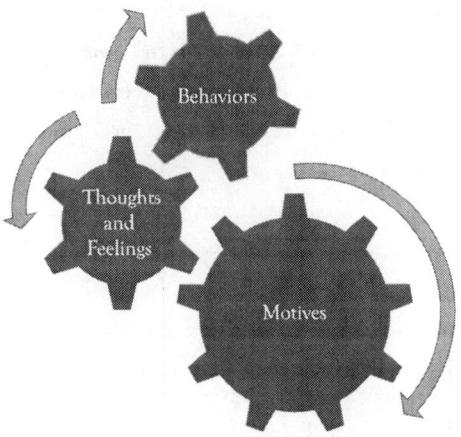

Another critical link in the chain between innate characteristics and their related behaviors is thoughts and feelings. McClelland, for example, describes motives as inner drives that shape the way we think and feel, which ultimately shape behavior.[17] Similarly, Goleman describes the link among thoughts, feelings, and behaviors as critical elements of emotional intelligence.[18]

This set of relationships raises another important consideration for leadership development: What is the best approach for you to acquire and develop leadership skills? Is it at the:

a) Behavioral level—meaning the acquisition and demonstration of certain knowledge and skills?
b) Thoughts and feelings level—changing what goes on inside the head and the heart?
c) Innate personality level—reengineering our basic drives or values?

From a trainability perspective, a behavioral approach to leadership development is the most pragmatic. This approach rests on the four essential elements of adult learning:[19]

1. *Recognition and understanding of the desired behaviors*
   It is important to identify the specific elements of the characteristic, competency, or skill in terms of what is observable and doable. For example, it is not sufficient to say that a leader needs to be a coach, which is a general description of the role. More specifically, the behavior is that the leader as coach meets routinely with each team member, provides ongoing feedback, and delegates specific tasks as development opportunities.
2. *Assessment*
   Assessing your behavior is how you have "skin in the game." Without an assessment, ideally with both self-feedback and feedback from others, you are more likely to intellectualize these as concepts rather than considering them in the context of your professional development.
3. *Practice*
   Practice is deliberate, painstaking, and methodical. It is an opportunity for an individual to experiment, push beyond one's comfort zone, take risks, make mistakes, learn, and try again. Practice with feedback is essential for changing behavior.
4. *Application*
   If practice takes place in the lab, application takes place in the real world. It is the demonstration of critical behaviors appropriately applied to people and situations to get desired outcomes. Applica-

tion of the right behavior at the right time for the desired outcome is the definition of successful leadership performance.

We are still left to consider how easily you can acquire these leadership behaviors. In order to be effective, the training and development process needs to take into consideration the level of effort needed to demonstrate the appropriate knowledge, skills, and behaviors effectively, and the extent to which these elements interrelate and reinforce each other. The more they interrelate, the easier it is to develop them in concert. There is also another consideration that has longer-term implications for the type of professional development needed to succeed in strategic leadership. What is the possibility that, through intensive, deliberate practice and development, the focus is not only on how you change behavior but also on how you *think and feel*, making it easier to sustain the behavior over time. Deliberate practice is something we will explore in Chapter 4 when examining the role of a leader as a coach and a teacher.

The point is that as a new or existing leader, the focus on leadership behavior is important because it gives you something that is specific, concrete, and doable, something you can practice and apply. But there's more that needs to happen. The longer-term benefit of professional development is the potential to change how you think. The more these behaviors connect together, the greater the opportunity to create a change in mindset and perspective. We begin with identifying the desired behaviors. We rely on the link between thinking and behavior to work in both directions: Changes in thinking can impact behavior; changes in behavior can impact thinking.

To What Extent Are There Identifiable Stages That Uniquely Characterize Leadership at Certain Points in One's Career?

The concept of development stages is one widely used in the field of psychology. A stage is characterized by distinct qualitative differences in thinking. Piaget in the field of cognitive development and Kohlberg in the field of moral development use stages to explain different reasoning patterns as children mature.[20] The process of moving from one stage to the next is a transformation for how an individual thinks, sees the world, and makes judgments.

For Kohlberg, stages had to meet certain criteria:

1. They represent qualitative differences in the way people think.
2. They are "structured wholes," meaning that they represent patterns of thinking that show up across a variety of issues.
3. They are hierarchically integrated, "that people do not lose the insights gained at lower stages, but integrate them into new, broader frameworks."[21]
4. They exist in "invariant sequence." This means that people progress through the stages from the first to the second to the third and so on.[22]

Additionally, there are two pioneers in the field of motivational research who utilize a hierarchical concept similar to stage development. In 1959, Frederick Herzberg, a renowned clinical psychologist, described two levels of motivators at work. At one level are hygiene or maintenance factors such as salary, work conditions, and security. At a higher level are job motivators, such as recognition, responsibility, advancement, and meaningful work. According to Herzberg, hygiene factors alone do not create job satisfaction, but their absence can create dissatisfaction. When hygiene factors are met at a lower level, the factors at the higher level are motivators for job satisfaction.[23]

Abraham Maslow's theory of motivation argues that an individual has certain hierarchical stages of needs, ranging from physiological and safety needs at a base level, to self-esteem and self-actualization at a higher level. Similar to Herzberg, Maslow's lower-level needs, also described as deficiency needs, are prominent in their absence. When these lower-level needs are satisfied, they create a base for growth in self-esteem and self-actualization.[24]

From the fields of psychology and motivational research, one can extract four unique benefits by using a stage concept for leadership development:

- First, stages define specific regions on a leadership development road map. Similar to the logic used by Piaget and Kohlberg, stages are hierarchically integrated, meaning that as you move into a new stage along the map, you retain the insights and experience from lower stages and integrate them into broader frameworks.

- Second, stages are heuristic models or "structured wholes" that represent patterns of thinking, unique role perspectives, skill requirements, and critical behaviors that apply across a variety of situations. As a leader at a particular stage of development, you think and act across a variety of situations through an integrated skill set.
- Third, stages give focus and direction to the development process. Specifically, stages are a more prescriptive approach for *when* and *how* you need to use certain leadership tools, techniques, and practices than simply drawing from a laundry list of attributes.
- Fourth, stages tell a story, where shifts and leaps, defying gravity and defining the third win, and evolution and revolution are all critical for successful outcomes.

Creating a Context for Leadership: Using Performance Standards

Earlier I mentioned that what is unique about leadership is how roles and responsibilities are defined, which impacts what leadership looks like in terms of expectations, situations, and competency application. These requirements can differ by position, function, organizational culture, type of business, or all the above. Therefore, to understand what leadership looks like for you requires understanding the context of your position, meaning what are the critical responsibilities and subsequent behaviors that define success. One method for understanding context is the use of performance standards. Performance standards are akin to a job analysis that human resource professionals use to scope out basic duties and responsibilities for a particular job or job family. For our purposes, performance standards need to answer three basic questions for a specific position:

- *What* does the job entail?
- *How* does a person perform the job?
- *Who* are the critical interfaces, meaning the people or groups with whom this position must interact with to perform effectively?

Defining the "What" and the "How": The Bartender

Performance standards
the job _____

Measures of success	Critical tasks	Technical skills	Critical behaviors

←— The what —→   ←— The how —→

To illustrate the performance standards process, imagine that you are an owner of a new pub in town and want to hire the *best* bartender. What does it mean to be *the best,* and what specifically are you looking for in terms of experience, knowledge, and skills?

The first step is to define what specifically the job is. The *what* consists of

a) *measures of success,* which are quantifiable outcome metrics. These measures could be the number of drinks served, revenue, profitability, customer satisfaction, and repeat business in some combination of factors;

b) *critical tasks.* Tasks are specific duties and responsibilities. For a bartender, the tasks are mixing drinks, greeting, and serving customers, stocking the bar, cleaning the bar, ordering inventory, and making change.

When you combine (a) the measures of success with (b) the critical tasks, the net result is a job description, a definition of what the job entails. The measures and tasks for *your* bartender depend on how you define the role and what you expect to see as outcomes.

The second step is to define the skill set, the *how.* This step requires the identification of:

c) *technical skills.* These refer to the job-specific, content-related aspect of the job. Generally speaking, they are often a mix of basic knowledge and skill requirements. For your bartender, the "technical" skills could include knowledge of drink recipes, basic knowledge of beer and wine, math skills, and use of the point of sale system;

d) *critical behaviors*. These behaviors, also described as competencies, are characteristics that define outstanding performance in the job. As the owner, you have an image of what special qualities you want for your bartender. Perhaps, it's mixing a great drink, having a great memory, and making a good appearance. You might want someone who is personable, tactful, and professional. While these characteristics are broad in scope, at some point, you will need to define them in observable and behavioral terms. For example, a great memory means that a bartender "addresses regular customers by their names as they enter the bar," or "remembers and delivers their favorite beverages."

When you combine (c) the technical skills and (d) the critical behaviors, the net result is the skill set, which also serves as a template for training and development.

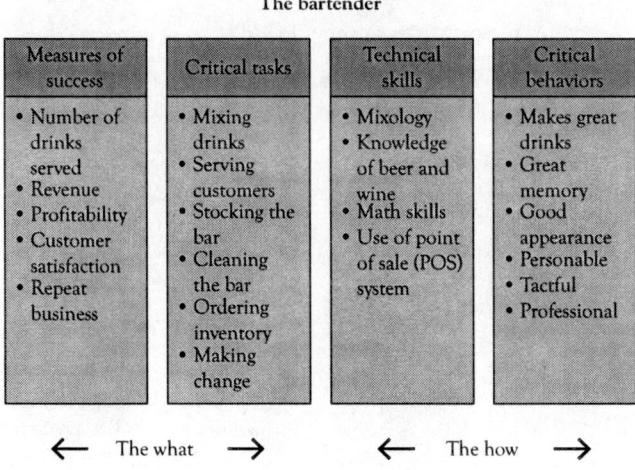

Performance standards
The bartender

Measures of success	Critical tasks	Technical skills	Critical behaviors
• Number of drinks served • Revenue • Profitability • Customer satisfaction • Repeat business	• Mixing drinks • Serving customers • Stocking the bar • Cleaning the bar • Ordering inventory • Making change	• Mixology • Knowledge of beer and wine • Math skills • Use of point of sale (POS) system	• Makes great drinks • Great memory • Good appearance • Personable • Tactful • Professional

← The what →   ← The how →

Defining "the Who": The Job Wheel

While the "bartender" analysis creates overall expectations for roles, responsibilities, and skill sets, it does not give a sense of priority, proportion, or timing. One method to determine these factors is the use of a job wheel. This is a process for deciding which interface—meaning which individuals and groups—are most critical for successful performance. The value of prioritizing interfaces is that it prescribes what relationships are most important to build and maintain, and it pinpoints what specific duties and tasks are required in those relationships. For the new leader and for the technical professional looking to achieve subject matter expert status, developing a game plan for key relationships is an essential component for building credibility individually and for the team.

The process begins by identifying the individuals or groups with whom this position must interface in order to execute the responsibilities successfully. For our bartender, those interfaces include customers, the wait staff, the owner, other bartenders, and vendors. Then it is a matter of deciding how critical each interface is to the bartender's overall performance. This is accomplished by rating each interface as A, B, or C. As are most critical; Bs, critical; and Cs, less critical. By going to each A interface and identifying the critical tasks needed, the result is a list of prioritized tasks and critical interfaces needed for successful performance.

If you are currently in a leadership position, you may need to go through the prioritization process twice—first, the priorities as they are *currently*; second, the priorities as they *should be* to maximize job effectiveness. You will notice in the following example that customers are rated as an A priority. You will also see that the business owner, currently listed

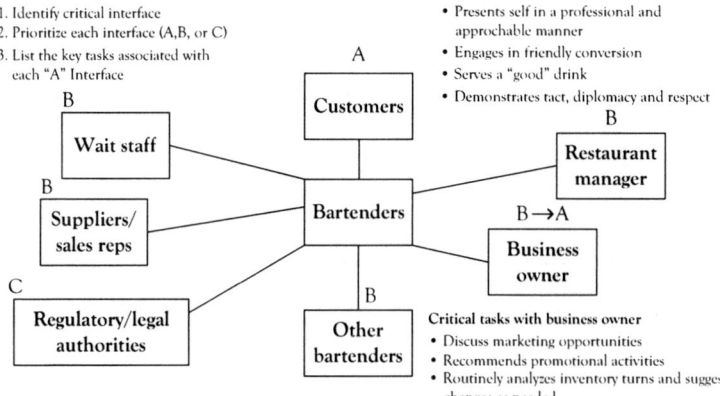

The job wheel process
Identifying the "who"

Instructions
1. Identify critical interface
2. Prioritize each interface (A, B, or C)
3. List the key tasks associated with each "A" Interface

Critical tasks with customers
• Presents self in a professional and approachable manner
• Engages in friendly conversion
• Serves a "good" drink
• Demonstrates tact, diplomacy and respect

A — Customers
B — Wait staff
B — Suppliers/sales reps
C — Regulatory/legal authorities
Bartenders
B — Other bartenders
B — Restaurant manager
B→A — Business owner

Critical tasks with business owner
• Discuss marketing opportunities
• Recommends promotional activities
• Routinely analyzes inventory turns and suggests changes as needed

as a B priority, is elevated to an A priority in thinking about the future. The reason is the desire for this bartender position to play a future role in increasing traffic into the bar, which means spending more time with the owner to consider more promotional activities and better management of the inventory.

Using the Job Wheel to Clarify Your Roles and Responsibilities

The use of the job wheel is an excellent process to clarify roles and responsibilities for the current job, future job, or both. This is particularly crucial for new leaders, yet existing leaders, particularly in the midst of shifts in business direction or priorities, can also benefit from this process.

First, create a blank job wheel on a sheet of paper. Brainstorm a list of critical interfaces for your position as you define it. Rate each interface in terms of current priority based on importance and time spent with each interface. Do this activity objectively and without value judgment. Lots of A priorities? This is not a problem at this point.

Second, determine what the priorities *should be* based on their importance to the successful execution of your roles and your responsibilities moving forward. (This step is most likely relevant to existing rather than new leaders.) Some interfaces could drop in priority, some escalate in importance, some will stay the same, and some might disappear altogether. While you may end up with several A priorities, they cannot all be As; some interfaces are more important than others to your job success. For each of the *should be* As, list out three to five critical tasks you need to perform with that individual or group.

Third is the clarification step. Sit down with your manager to discuss your job wheel and prioritized interfaces, both current and future, along with your rationale. Having the wheel with your prioritizations as a visual representation sparks the right discussion needed to bring clarity and agreement about your job.

Once the priorities and tasks are determined, you can then move to the bartender diagram, using the critical tasks as an anchor to completing measures, technical skills, and critical behaviors.

This process of rating each interface is a simple yet impactful method for setting priorities. The key is to get the right people involved in determining not just what these roles are, but what they *should be*. While some people may not agree, every interface can't be an A priority. When every interface is an "A," the jobs tend to be fragmented and unfocused. Some interfaces are more important than others. Forcing definition of the right "A" interfaces brings clarity to the job and sets priorities and expectations for performance, particularly in terms of what the job needs to look like moving forward.

To recap this section, the performance standards process, by intent, is an organic method for defining roles and responsibilities. It facilitates an ongoing dialogue for setting and managing expectations. Using the process as a combination of the bartender and job wheel activities creates a relationship among the what, the how, and the who of the job.

The Mentoré Leadership Competency Model

A Leadership Development Road map: Background and Rationale

With a method for bringing clarity to leadership roles and responsibilities in hand, the next requirement is a developmental road map to define what skills, competencies, and behaviors are needed as you become more seasoned and as your leadership and impact broaden across the business. Using an appropriately constructed competency model is a proven method for creating such a road map, identifying behavioral standards, and setting expectations.

At the time I began my consulting career, the field of competency research was beginning to take off.[25] The term "competency" had a specialized meaning—"an underlying characteristic of a person which enables them to deliver superior performance in a given job, role, or situation."[26] The basis for the research, spearheaded by Dr. David McClelland, Harvard professor, and several of his protégés, was to identify the characteristics of the best performers, to understand what they thought and did more often, in greater combination, and for more effective results than average performers.

It was not long before there was an explosion of interest in the field. The term competency was used broadly to mean everything from a basic skill to a unique way of thinking or pattern of behavior. Competency models, which are constellations of competencies intended to define successful performance in a particular job or role, were popping up everywhere. It was not unusual to see a model with 25 or more competency headings and more than a hundred behavioral indicators. I know this to be true because I created some of these myself. And with the advent of technology and Internet capability, what I saw was a commoditization of creating competencies and competency models rather than as a specialized discipline.

Eventually what this signaled to me was a renewed interest and focus with clients on *how* competencies and competency models are *used* as opposed to how they are cre-

> *Some people try to find things in the game that don't exist but football to me is only two things—blocking and tackling.*
> *Vince Lombardi*

ated. My particular goal was to create a simplified model that could be used primarily for leadership development. My criteria was that the model has to be relevant, actionable, pragmatic, and uncomplicated. I wanted it to explain how behaviors, thought processes, and perspectives can exist as integrated wholes or stages of development. It needed to be a road map, not a laundry list. And, it had to tell a compelling story, one that people would remember, use, and tell other people. This was the rationale for creating the Mentoré model.[27]

Dimensions of Effective Leadership

Job Expertise

Understanding the skill and behavioral characteristics of effective leadership starts by getting a general lay of the land, looking for major characteristics and features that define the overall landscape. What we know is that the practice of leadership to this point has benefited from a two-dimensional model or road map that consists of managing tasks and relationships.[28] From a skill acquisition and development perspective, task-related performance is measured by job expertise. As mentioned earlier, the use of the term "expertise" is used broadly to describe skill proficiency and applied knowledge in the content-based requirements of any job. As we will explore more in the next chapter, expertise can refer to either the attainment of a specific level or standard, or to an ongoing process for knowledge and skill mastery. Expertise is necessary for leadership success, but as we will see, it is not what differentiates superior from average performance.[29]

Relationship Management

The second dimension, relationship-related behavior, is made up of a unique skill set focused on understanding people. Successful relationships are fueled by building credibility, the extent to which *others* attribute value to you. Relationship-related behaviors are often associated with the leadership concepts of motivation, communication, influence, and collaboration. The combination of expertise and relationship management creates a solid leadership base. Moving into more strategic positions, however, requires one additional factor.

Business Savvy

Today there is an added element needed to survey the landscape better, and that is the ability to see the bigger picture and look farther down the road. Unfortunately, the rate of change challenges organizations to think longer term, especially when there is a less-than-certain forward direction. The hopes for a steady-state and prolonged stability are yesterday's dreams. Focus and priority are hard to come by. Communication and alignment are OK at best. The battle cry to the troops has been to work smarter, not harder. Unfortunately, the troops are too busy to work smarter.

While the focus on job-based expertise and relationship management provides situational guidance for leadership, the combination comes up short in today's business environment, especially since direction, focus, and priority are daily requirements. Perhaps, Burns and Bass saw this coming 30 years ago when they described the need for transformational leadership, the need for vision, and the ability to see the big picture that is needed to provide guidance and direction.[30]

In terms of leadership requirements, the big picture refers to understanding the business and the context in which your role exists. It means knowing what business you are in, how it's organized, how it derives value and profitability, what the current and future drivers for success are, and, importantly, how you fit in. How big is "*big*"? That answer depends on where you sit in the organization. The picture widens as you move from a team, to a functional, to an enterprise perspective. Ultimately, the big picture includes external customers, competitors, and the marketplace, both currently and in the future.

What fuels the ability to see and understand the big picture is strategic thinking. When strategic thinking is linked to job-related competence and relationship management, it creates a three-dimensional model that defines what leadership competencies and behaviors are most critical to meet the challenges and complexities in today's business environment, and what's needed to compete in the future. When strategic thinking is uniquely applied to the business, it creates a new type of intelligence characterized as "business savvy."

Leadership dimensions

Deriving Leadership Competencies

What is the overall context in which leadership is needed in today's business environment? There are conditions created by how the opposing forces of connectivity and fragmentation collide on a daily basis. Technology and globalization create connectivity, while the rate of change and volume of information create fragmentation. If leadership is anything, it is dynamic. By necessity, leadership is both situational, what's most effective in a specific situation, and transformational, what's important given the overall vision and direction. Leadership is calculus, not algebra. It requires continuous calibration. The fact that leadership is dynamic, however, does not mean that it is random. Using a competency model as a road map is one means for creating a level of predictability and expectations sequenced along a progression of stages, each with complementary roles, unique perspectives, important tasks, and critical behaviors.

The ability for a competency model to serve as a developmental road map is shaped not only by which competencies and behaviors are needed, but how they relate to each other in terms of thought process, perspective, and focus. By design, the Mentoré model represents an evolution of leadership, from building personal competence to expanding organizational capacity, from asking what and who to how and why, and moving from knowledge-based expertise to strategic leadership. Strategic leadership does not refer simply to those individuals at the executive level. It refers to the type of leadership that people need in numerous types of positions up and down the organization responsible for working *on* the business, far beyond just technical know-how and day-to-day execution.

The Mentoré model consists of four stages. Each stage consists of four competencies. When linked together within each stage, the competencies represent a distinct perspective, focus, role, and set of behaviors. Following is an overview of the model with brief descriptors of each competency.

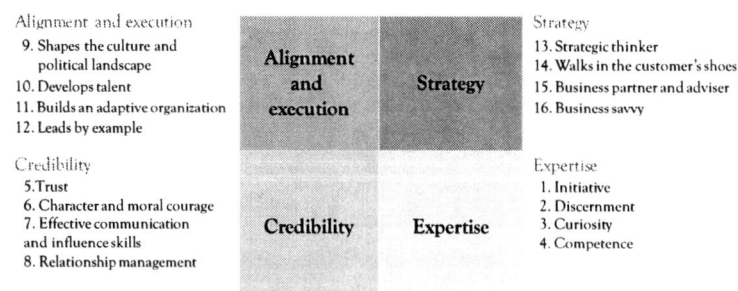

The mentoré leadership competency model

Alignment and execution
9. Shapes the culture and political landscape
10. Develops talent
11. Builds an adaptive organization
12. Leads by example

Strategy
13. Strategic thinker
14. Walks in the customer's shoes
15. Business partner and adviser
16. Business savvy

Credibility
5. Trust
6. Character and moral courage
7. Effective communication and influence skills
8. Relationship management

Expertise
1. Initiative
2. Discernment
3. Curiosity
4. Competence

Stage One: Expertise

Stage overview   Expertise is the starting point for development. It is based on job content and technical proficiency and a track record of successful performance. Expertise is a potent mix of drive, intellect, and experience.

In the expertise stage you spend your time building a base of knowledge, learning the ropes, getting a lay of the land in terms of processes and procedures, developing and refining your ability to think analytically, diving below the surface of a problem or looking beyond the obvious, driving for and getting results, perhaps leading a project or two, getting as smart as you can about everything related to the work itself, and continuously striving for mastery of the critical knowledge and experience in your job. In a nutshell, you're looking, digging, learning, and achieving results.

The expertise competencies are

1. **initiative:** the energy, drive, and determination to get results;
2. **discernment:** the ability to think analytically and make informed judgments—to reason and comprehend, particularly about what is not apparent;
3. **curiosity:** a hunger to learn, explore, and dig deeper, especially to make sense out of uncertainty;
4. **competence:** mastery and proficiency—the ability to apply knowledge and skills that consistently achieve outcomes to prescribed standards in a variety of circumstances and situations.

Stage Two: Credibility

Stage overview   Credibility is built on one's ability to commit and deliver value to others. It is the basis for developing and managing relationships. It is an important stage for a new leader, and is also critical for the technical professional looking to achieve technical status as a subject matter expert and potentially moving farther along on a technical track.

With a base of expertise under your belt, you make a conscious shift in priorities. Beyond just getting results, you realize the value of what it means to commit and deliver to others and build a track record of success.

In this stage, you spend your time building relationships, learning what's important to the people around you, increasing your visibility in the organization, building a reputation as someone who uses your knowledge and skill to help others solve their problems and reach their goals, learning and practicing effective communication skills and "the art of persuasion,"[31] developing your own networks, and creating an image as a person of character, integrity, and courage.

The credibility competencies are

5. **relationship management:** establishing rapport, making connections, building relationships, and creating networks critical to both short- and long-term goals;
6. **character and moral courage:** the demonstration of integrity and the highest professional standards even when facing adversity or making the tough decisions—how you choose to do business;
7. **credibility and trust:** building a positive reputation based on your ability to commit and deliver value to others;
8. **effective communication and influence skills:** the ability to listen, to communicate at the level of the audience, and to persuade others effectively by identifying common ground and striving for mutually beneficial outcome.

Stage Three: Alignment and Execution

Stage overview   Alignment and execution are working through others to maximize performance and deliver results. Both new and existing leaders move into this stage at some point once they have a base of credibility and continue to build upon it.

Up to this point your ability to execute effectively is because of your direct hands-on ability—brains, brawn, and results. Additionally, maybe you have had success in leading a small project team of colleagues, managing a college intern for the summer, or having a junior associate report to you. Moving into the stage of alignment and execution, however, is different. In this stage, the organization or business, needs and expects you to translate your personal capability into organizational capacity each and every day. Your role may be one of directly managing others, or it could be as a project manager or technical contributor with expanded responsibilities for cross-functional activities. In all cases, your value is limited by hands-on involvement yet expanded by your ability to achieve results through others.

In this stage, you spend your time aligning and realigning processes and priorities with duties and responsibilities, increasing the effectiveness of the team, clarifying roles and responsibilities, setting expectations, developing talent, coaching and teaching, influencing the decision-making process, expanding your networks, leading change initiatives, and modeling the behavior that you expect from others.

The alignment and execution competencies

9. **shape the culture and political landscape:** shapes a culture based on mutual respect, trust, and accountability;
10. **build an adaptive organization:** creates a high-performance organization that gets results by continually aligning strategy, roles, skill sets, and leadership responsibilities;
11. **develop talent:** takes pride in role as coach and teacher who get the most out of individuals and teams;
12. **lead by example:** models the leadership behaviors and values expected of others.

Stage Four: Strategy

Stage overview As a stage in leadership development, strategy means being strategic and engaging in strategic leadership. Being strategic requires looking out beyond organizational or functional boundaries to understand the bigger picture and business. For managers of people, strategic leadership is a combination of managing at least a part of the business organization, thinking strategically, and developing business acumen, which leadership expert Ram Charan describes as "the keen awareness of how money is made."[32] For technical professionals, strategic leadership is a combination of ongoing technical expertise combined with strategic thinking and business acumen. In both cases, leaders who operate at this level are valuable not only because of their experience and insight, but also because they have the foresight to lead the business into the future.

In this stage, you spend your time looking outside your organization to see the bigger picture, learning what's important to both internal and external customers, forging partnerships across the enterprise, and understanding the business and how it derives value and profitability.

The strategy competencies are as follows:

13. **Strategic thinker:** the ability to see the big picture by thinking broadly and extrapolating from current to future trends and outcomes
14. **Walks in the customer's shoes:** creates and develops a customer dialogue that can involve all levels of the organization.
15. **Business partner and strategist:** works as partner and positions the organization to deliver value through ongoing commitment and shared risk for the success of the end-customer—strives for win–win–win outcomes
16. **Business savvy:** understands how the business makes money—takes the risks and creates opportunities needed to remain viable as a business entity

Skin in the Game

Preassessment Activity

One way to maximize the value of what is to follow in this book is to do a short assessment of where you see yourself in terms of these stages, which competencies are most important to you now, and what's critical as you move forward in the next 12 months. Take 15 minutes to answer these questions:

1. Which of the four stages—expertise, credibility, alignment and execution, and strategy—best characterizes where you are *currently* spending your time?
   Current stage: _____
   What are three to five major responsibilities in which you are currently engaged?

- _____
- _____
- _____
- _____
- _____

2. In which stage do you think you *should be* spending your time in the next 12 months?

   Stage where you *should be*: _____

   If this is not where you currently are, what will it take for you to get there? List three activities you need to do *more of*, and three activities you need to do *less of.*

More of	Less of

3. Look through the competencies and their descriptions again.
   - Which of these are *most* important for your current success? Why? Choose no more than eight.
   - Which of these are *most* important to you in the next 12 months? Why? Choose no more than eight.

Competency	Current importance (check no more than 8)	Importance in the next 12 months (check no more than 8)	Rationale
Expertise stage			
Initiative			
Discernment			
Curiosity			
Competence			

Credibility stage Trust Character and moral courage Effective communication and influence skills Relationship management			
Alignment and execution stage Shapes the culture and political landscape Develops talent Builds an adaptive organization Leads by example			
Strategy stage Strategic thinker Walks in the customer's shoes Business partner and strategist Business savvy			

4. Consider meeting with your manager to discuss your responses and ratings and to get her feedback. This is a great opportunity to discuss your professional development in the context of leadership stages and competencies.

5. Think of this preassessment as a snapshot, by no means a complete picture as yet for your leadership development. Use it as a reference point as you read through the next chapters to ask yourself if you are spending your time working in the right areas, developing the right skills, and thinking about the right things.

Chapter Summary

Taking Stock

- At its most basic level, leadership is the ability to influence the way people think and feel to the point they take decisive and responsible action.

- Historically, leadership was defined as innate traits and characteristics. By the mid-20th century, researchers studied leadership in terms of behavior in specific situations. Today leadership theory has continued to evolve into the study of effective leadership behavior. While traits are innate and difficult to develop, behaviors are observable and more easily trained and developed.
- Leadership occurs within a context of a particular business, organization, and job. The use of performance standards and the job wheel process are tools to define what the job is, the skill and behavioral expectations for how the job is performed, and the most critical individuals or group with whom this job must interface to perform successfully.
- Two research trends help define a road map for leadership development:

  o Competency research identifies those characteristics and behaviors indicative of outstanding performance. Part of the success of constructing a competency model is its ability to tell a story.
  o Stage development, used in the fields of psychological and motivational research, creates a framework of "structured wholes, identify qualitative differences in thinking patterns, and integrate insights gained from lower stages into higher ones."

- The three dimensions that define leadership are technical competence, relationship management, and being business savvy.
- The Mentoré leadership competency model incorporates these three dimensions into a road map for leadership development. It consists of four stages: expertise, credibility, alignment and execution, and strategy. At a conceptual level, the model is a heuristic device to describe and consider the essential thought processes and beliefs inside effective leadership. From a behavioral level, the model identifies a set of integrated competencies for taking action.

CHAPTER 2

Stage One: Expertise

Building a Base

Life in the Vortex

Imagine that you are a marketing manager who just hired Sarah Richman, a recent college graduate, for a new position, one to improve the company's social media presence. What impressed you most about her is the raw talent you saw—a mix of drive and intellect. So it comes as no surprise that after a couple of weeks on the job, Sarah wants to sit down with you to get your advice. She understands her role. That part she got from the interview process and your first meeting with her when she arrived. What she wants to understand is what you think she has to do to be successful. You tell her to "work hard, use her head, learn a lot, and do a good job." It sounds good, but she tells you that her parents gave her that advice three years ago when she worked her first summer job. She tries the question again, "What do I need to know and do in order to execute my role effectively?" She wants to understand what it will take for her to be the best, and she is asking you to coach her, to really explain to her what she needs to learn, how she needs to be thinking about things, and what she needs to do. She just validated your ability to spot drive and intellect. How do you answer Sarah's question?

Maybe you are thinking that you have never had this happen before and would give anything to have such an employee. However, I contend that this discussion, more likely a series of discussions, is one you want to have whether someone asks for it or not. Yes, it is about working hard, using your head, learning a lot, and doing a good job, but it needs to be framed in learning and mastering the fundamentals for building a base of expertise.

Expertise

Expertise stage

Expertise is the first stage in leadership development and is focused on learning the content of the job and applying the knowledge to achieve results.

Expertise competencies

Initiative: *the energy, drive, and determination to get results*

Discernment: *the ability to think analytically and make informed judgments—to reason and comprehend, particularly about what is not apparent*

Curiosity: *a hunger to learn, explore, and dig deeper, especially to make sense out of uncertainty*

Competence: *mastery and proficiency—the ability to apply knowledge and skills that consistently achieve outcomes to prescribed standards in a variety of circumstances and situations*

To a great extent, expertise is based on knowledge, and if you believe Sir Francis Bacon, *Scientia potential est—knowledge is power.*[1] However, there is more than just the knowledge itself that is important for building expertise. There is a need to understand what someone sees as important, how he or she thinks and acquires knowledge, and how that knowledge is applied. This takes us to understanding the concepts of motivation, thinking, and learning.

Understanding Motivation

Motivation is a topic that has intrigued everyone from psychologists to writers to Monday morning quarterbacks. Earlier we examined how researchers like Maslow[2] and Herzberg[3] relate motivation to a set of intrinsic needs, some basic and primal in nature, and others associated with psychological growth and development. Also prominent in the study of motivation is Harvard professor and mentor to other experts in the field, David McClelland. McClelland wrote *The Achieving Society* in 1961 to examine the role that motivation plays in economic development. McClelland describes different types of social motives, motives that drive our behavior in interactions with others.[4]

McClelland's discovery is that each of us possesses three sources of motivational energy. Each source has a particular focus, and drives us to fulfill a particular intrinsic need:

- **Power** is focused on *people* to have *a positive impact* on others
- **Achievement** is focused on *tasks* to perform work *efficiently and effectively*
- **Affiliation** is also focused on *people* to create *close, personal relationships*

The Power Motive

Is power good or bad? As basic motivation, power is neither. What makes us think power is good or bad depends on how it is used. McClelland clearly understood this distinction.[5] Think of the best boss you have ever seen or had. People describe a good teacher, someone who is approachable, who values them for their contributions, is firm but fair, is a good coach, shares the credit, and is a good listener. McClelland characterized this type of power as socialized for positive, win–win outcomes. These individuals demonstrate self-control, have strong values, and empower others.[6]

Think of the worst boss. Some of the more common responses are micromanager, manipulative, looking out for #1, intimidating, inconsistent, and my personal favorite—the Teflon manager, someone who takes the credit but let's the blame just slide off. McClelland describes this type of power as personalized: ego-driven, self-serving, and manipulative. Personalized power is power without self-control, and the need to impact others is calculated and manipulative, to look good at any cost.[7]

Power is the motive of *influence*. The thought process created by the power motive is how to impact others, to make a favorable impression. These thoughts are linked to behaviors such as

- wanting to be in charge;
- coaching and motivating others;
- teaching and giving advice;
- achieving work through others;
- displaying pictures or objects that suggest prestige or status;
- wanting to win;
- engaging in politics on or off the job;
- networking and "working the room."

The Achievement Motive

Achievement is the motive of accomplishing work as *efficiently and effectively* as possible. Since the focus is on the task, the value that achievement derives is to do the best job possible.

The thought process linked to achievement is one of accomplishing goals to an internal set of standards of excellence. Characteristic behaviors include

- taking initiative;
- doing new and exciting work;
- working independently to get the most done;
- working collaboratively if it involves working with other smart, motivated people, meaning other high achievers;
- seeking performance-related feedback;
- looking for ways to maximize efficiencies and avoid waste;
- wanting to demonstrate how much you know, how smart you are;
- craving for challenges and accomplishing something new;
- getting results.

The Affiliation Motive

Affiliation, like power, focuses on people. But affiliation has no agenda and no need to impact others. Affiliation fulfills the need to create close, social relationships.

Affiliation is the motive of *personal connections*. The thought process is one in which creating and maintaining those connections is vital. It's about reaching out to others, to create personal relationships that span both work and personal life.

The types of behaviors associated with affiliation are

- preferring to work with friends and in teams;
- consoling others, particularly during difficult times;
- socializing with coworkers both on and off the job;
- embracing the good times and avoiding conflicts;
- keeping pictures of family, pets, and friends in sight;
- keeping in touch with former colleagues;
- wanting to be liked and accepted.

Understanding Your Motivational Profile

Based on the descriptions for power, achievement, and affiliation, how do you characterize your motivation?

Create a profile by drawing a set of bar graphs, one for each motive. Use a **total** of 20 points to distribute across the three motives like the ensuing example.

Keep in mind there is no right answer, nor should you expect that you are equal in all three.

Example

Motivational profile

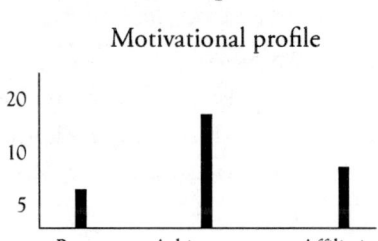

Is there one particular motive that is highest? Lowest? What does your profile say about what's important to you and how you think? What types of behaviors are easiest for you to demonstrate? More difficult to demonstrate?

> Your motivational profile represents *a starting point* for what's import-
> ant to you, how you think, and what you do. While your motive profile
> basically remains the same, through conscious thought and practice you
> can adopt or change certain motive-related behaviors.

According to McClelland, each of us possesses these motives to different levels. Said another way, each of us has a unique, personal profile of power, achievement, and affiliation. Understanding this motivational profile is a way to understand what is *important* to each of us. There is no "right" motive profile: We are who we are. As we discussed in the previous chapter, motives link to certain behaviors. Understanding your own motivation, therefore, helps identify your starting point or inclination about what comes naturally and what is more difficult. While changing your underlying basic motivation is very difficult, it is possible to change your behavior, such as adopting a new skill that may not come naturally to you. We use this premise in leadership development all the time. For example, networking with others or "working the room" may not come naturally to you, but you can learn to do them effectively. Such changes take conscious thought, practice, and feedback. Over time, these behaviors become more natural and expected, which suggests that there could be changes in how you think about them and their importance.

McClelland cuts a wide path for understanding motivation, and his insights are important to understand the link between what motivates us, how we think, and what we do. As we look at building expertise, it is easy to see the link between achievement motivation and how it relates to acquiring knowledge. Achievement is a driver for learning, particularly as fuel for "working hard and doing a good job." Achievement also pushes the standards, sets the bar, and causes craving for performance-based feedback. These elements play an important role in both the acquisition and application of knowledge. The power motive is relevant in the discussion of leadership as influence. Affiliation plays an important role in empathy. Both the power and affiliation motives will be explored in the next chapter.

The Process of Thinking and Learning: A Fundamental Element in Leadership Development

Thinking about thinking is a fundamental component for effective leadership development. While there is a long history of theories in the fields of psychology and philosophy for how we think and learn, there are three contemporary researchers whose concepts are particularly relevant to the field of leadership development. First is Howard Gardner.[8] Gardner's early research is based on the concept that each of us has multiple intelligences rather than one indicated by the general measure for intellectual capacity. Gardner defined seven intelligences as the linguistic, logical-mathematical, musical, bodily kinesthetic, spatial-visual, interpersonal, and intrapersonal. Each intelligence represents "the way in which one carries out a task in virtue of one's goals."[9] More recently, Gardner turned his attention to five types of thinking that are needed in the future.[10] He refers to these types as *minds*, meaning different capacities or perspectives. Each mind links behaviors and actions with a particular thought process:

1. A disciplined mind to be expert in at least one area
2. A synthesizing mind to put disparate pieces of information together and communicate them effectively
3. A creative mind first to build the box, then to think outside of it
4. A respectful mind to embrace diversity
5. An ethical mind to think beyond our own interests and to do what is right[11]

Gardner's framework is important for two reasons. First is its general application to the process of leadership development. Different minds create different perspectives, and these perspectives broaden leadership effectiveness across the development process. Second, Gardner's disciplined mind is a fundamental part of the expertise stage, and it lends credibility to why expertise is critical.

Another leader in the field is Chris Argyris. Argyris's interest is the connection between the actions people take and the thought processes behind them. He created two categories to explain how people characterize theories of action. One is how people describe what they do (espoused theory), and the second is what people actually do (theory in use). What interests Argyris is the extent to which what people espouse and what they do align to each other. That capacity is *reflection*.[12]

What Argyris finds most telling about how we think is when we detect an error or when something is not working out. In other words, how do we reconcile when the outcome from taking action does not match our intent? Here he finds two characteristic responses. One is that people change the *action* but stick to the original assumptions. He calls this approach single-loop learning. The second type is to question the underlying *assumptions* behind the actions taken. This questioning pattern is double-loop learning. Double-loop learning requires a deeper dive, greater reflection, and a willingness to question underlying assumptions.[13] The relevance of Argyris to our discussion is the flexibility in thinking that is required at different points in the development process. Sometimes, it's a matter of changing what actions we take; at other times it's a matter of changing how we frame the situation and the underlying assumptions.

Unlike Gardner and Argyris, Daniel Pink falls outside traditional academia, but his interests and research into how we think are deep inside the contemporary dialogue of what's needed for personal development and economic success.[14] Pink, a former White House speechwriter and current author, describes how traditional left-brain thinking, the side of the brain that handles logic, detail, sequence, and analysis, was an important aspect in the Information Age of the 20th century. However, Pink contends that right-brain thinking, the side of the brain that handles emotional expression, synthesis, context, and the big picture, needs to drive our thinking in the 21st century, the Conceptual Age. *Why?* While left-brain thinking is indispensable, it is no longer sufficient to thrive in a highly connected yet fragmented world. Rather, we need to think in terms of high concept, the ability to create artistic and emotional beauty, and high touch, the need for empathy and meaning, to live and contribute in today's society.[15]

To this end, Pink describes a future mindset of six senses:[16]

- Design: something that is emotionally engaging, not just functional
- Story: looking at characters and narrative in a situation, not just argument

- Symphony: the need for synthesis and the big picture, not just focus
- Empathy: the personal connection, not just logic
- Play: the levity and joy it brings, not just seriousness
- Meaning: seeking purpose and fulfillment

Pink gives us another framework for thinking about thinking. It stands to reason that building expertise is based on logic, analysis, and detail, and

> *Thinking about thinking is a fundamental component for effective leadership development.*

this need does not evaporate. However, the challenge that Pink presents is an immediate need to engage the other side of the brain as well. Expertise requires left-brain thinking, but the ability to engage these six senses creates a benefit for building broader intelligence that begins now and carries over into the other leadership developmental stages.

The relationship of motivation, thinking and learning, perspective taking, and behavior are central themes throughout the development process. The starting point for seeing how these elements tie together is the expertise stage.

Building a Base of Expertise

Like one of thousands of students who migrated to Boston in the early 1970s, I was sucked into the running craze that was hitting the nation. Inspired by Boston's own Bill Rogers, I bought my first pair of running shoes and started running the familiar loops around Jamaica Pond, Chestnut Hill Reservoir, and of course, the Charles River. I developed a steady diet of two miles, which eventually led to a couple of 5 kilometer fun runs. There I learned the difference between joggers and runners. Joggers run for fun and stop at water stations; runners run for time and grab water on the go. Over the course of next several years, I worked up to running 10 kilometer races, and by that point, I had several training buddies who had their eyes on the same prize: running a marathon. Since the Boston marathon requires a qualifying time and intense training in the darkness of New England winters, we agreed to train for a fall marathon in Newport, Rhode Island. I had also moved to Rhode Island, so the choice was a no-brainer.

One of my colleagues had a three-month marathon training plan created by a local track coach and marathoner himself, or so I was told. It was handwritten on a single sheet of paper that was a copy of a copy at least 10 times over. This was not a plan to go from 0 to 26.2 miles in three months. While there were specific workouts for the last 90 days, the plan rested on one important premise: the need to build a base, which, in this case, was 40 miles a week. First, build a base, and then use a structured plan to master the distance.[17]

Like running a marathon, successful leadership requires building a base, a base of expertise. Unfortunately, this is not as simple as grabbing a training schedule from a friend and following it for a few months. Expertise answers Sarah's question: "What do I need to know and do in order to execute my role effectively?" Expertise is the stage in leadership development focused on learning the content of the job and applying the knowledge to achieve results. It rests on four critical competencies. Separately each is important, and collectively they create a platform upon which additional knowledge, skills, and experiences are built. These competencies are

> **initiative:** the energy, drive, and determination to get results;

> **discernment:** the ability to think analytically and make informed judgments—to reason and comprehend, particularly about what is not apparent;

> **curiosity:** a hunger to learn, explore, and dig deeper, especially to make sense out of uncertainty;

> **competence:** mastery and proficiency—the ability to apply knowledge and skills that consistently achieve outcomes to prescribed standards in a variety of circumstances and situations.

Initiative

Initiative is intrinsic motivation. It is fueled by the need to achieve, just as McClelland describes it. In its rawest form, initiative is also attitude. It's drive with a dash of restlessness. It's in hot pursuit of getting work accomplished and taking charge of the situation when needed. Initiative is will with persistence. What makes initiative a vital component for building expertise is the energy and desire to take action and drive for results.[18]

Discernment

Discernment is a thinking process that exists at several different levels. At one level, discernment is analytical thinking. It's the ability to apply logic and reason to solving problems. It's understanding what's inside the box and how the pieces fit together. For example, several years ago, I had a car mechanic, Roger. I was having trouble starting my car and managed to drive in to his garage. He poked around and told me to leave the car with him overnight. He assured me that he would find and fix the problem because "no car could outsmart him." Roger was able to think under the hood. The final score: Roger 1, Car 0. Roger the warrior; Roger the analytical thinker.

One of the more common illustrations of analytical thinking is the use of the scientific method, something that we were encouraged to develop and use as a default mechanism since grade school. As we know, the scientific method is a specific set of interrelated steps to define the problem, create a hypothesis, collect data, test the hypothesis, and draw conclusions. What makes the scientific method work is the use of a consistent methodology based on structure, logic, and analytical thinking. It has rigor and discipline. The analytical thought process scales. We use it to think through a variety of situations from geometry to history, weather forecasting to party planning, landscaping the front yard to fixing cars. The scientific method as a problem-solving framework is a good friend.

One aspect of analytical thinking worth singling out is its ability to see relationships and make connections, such as determining cause and effect, or understanding the relationship between the whole and its parts. Additionally, it has the potential to construct, destruct, and reconstruct the elements of a problem and to search for solutions that are not readily apparent. As an individual moves through the leadership development process, the ability to make connections and see relationships broadens in scope across people, organizations, and the outside world.

At a deeper level, analytical thinking is about sharpening one's intellectual capacity. A part of this process is the ability to make informed judgments. This is discernment, the ability to see and understand situations clearly and intelligently. Consistently solving problems creates a good batting average. But to hit home runs takes *insight*, which is the ability to discern meaning and figure things out at a deeper level.

In the pursuit of framing and substantiating a judgment, there are several processes at work: the powers of observation, the collection of data, and the weighing of evidence. What is important is not simply the pursuit, but the ability to *step back* and *get perspective* on the situation:

- What's going on here?
- What do I "see"?
- What does this mean?
- What might I be missing?
- If I were to change places and look from another angle, what might be different?
- What am I learning?

The various ways by which we solve problems are indicative of how we think and learn. Consider the concept of single-loop and double-loop learning that Argyris describes.[19] When a problem occurs and a solution doesn't work, single-loop learning questions the actions that were taken. On the other hand, double-loop learning questions the assumptions that underlie the actions. It dives below the surface of *solving* the problem to *understand* what is going on. Both types of learning are important, but it's knowing when and how to use them that is critical. The ability to step back, take stock, test assumptions, and gain insight is the value that discernment brings to the overall process of thinking and learning. Moving forward, this ability only intensifies.

Curiosity

"What if…?"

What discernment is to thinking logically, curiosity is to thinking creatively. Curiosity has two sides. One side accepts, meaning it embraces new ideas and diverse perspectives. On the other side, it confronts. It questions authority, takes risks, and challenges perceived constraints. Curiosity is an itch that must be scratched. And when curiosity is unleashed, it has the power to create scientific breakthroughs and artistic triumphs. It is reason, and it is passion. For all these reasons, it is a critical competency needed for leadership.

What makes curiosity important in the expertise stage is its natural inquisitiveness with questions that come in all shapes and sizes. For certain they include what and how. But what curiosity seems to fuel is an insatiable need to go beyond why to contemplate, *what if ...?* Sometimes it's illuminating, and sometimes it's edgy. Sometimes it leads to understanding; sometimes, it leads to confusion.

Curiosity is nothing if not relentless. The need to ask questions is critical to the pursuit of acquiring and applying knowledge and skills, and building a base of expertise. However, it is not bound by logic. It speaks to Gardner's concept of the creative mind.[20] It has right-brained emotion and creativity, plus several of the senses that Pink describes, such as story, play, and meaning.[21]

The relationship of curiosity and discernment—inquisitiveness and judgment—creates a unique dynamic. They are a bit like the odd couple.[22] One is convergent—analyzing clues, making judgments, drawing conclusions—all neat and tidy. The other is divergent—asking questions, looking for options, wondering what if—messy and scattered. But they have figured out how to live together. Independently, each is important, but together they create a disciplined yet flexible way of thinking that is conducive to building a solid base of expertise.

Competence

Competence, also thought of as mastery or proficiency, is critical to building a base of expertise. When the term technical competence is used, it usually refers to the specific content in a chosen technical or scientific field, sometimes thought of as domain knowledge. The true test of competence is the ability to apply knowledge and skills that *consistently* achieves outcomes to prescribed standards in a variety of circumstances and situations.

Competence looks different based on several factors:

- *Differences based on professions*
  A competent nuclear engineer is different from competent trainer of border collies: different standards, different skill sets, and different outcomes.
- *Differences based on type and maturity of the business*
  In a small, entrepreneurial organization, for example, competent means the ability to oversee all aspects of the business. In a large multinational complex organization, competent could refer to highly specialized experience in a specific area, like international tax codes.
- *Differences based on depth of knowledge*
  At Almo Pharma, for example, an engineer 1 is expected to master one automation platform, while an engineer 2 must master two platforms.
- *Differences based on depth of knowledge* and *breadth of experience*
  Back at Almo Pharma, to reach the senior 3 engineer position, a senior 2 must have subject matter expertise in one specialty *and* 10 years of broad experience working in all other technical specialties across the department.

Measuring Competence

There are two schools of thought about what it means to be competent. One is that competence is an *end-state* reached by meeting predetermined, professional standards. This method relies on external standards to measure the level of proficiency. Another school of thought is that competence is the *process* of increasing proficiency. In this school, the value is not so much the diploma but the intrinsic motivation for learning and getting smarter along the way.[23]

One external method used to designate a desired level of competence is the use of licenses, tests, and professional certifications. This method requires the use of agreed-upon, objective standards to enter a profession and to stay up to date. For example, to become a certified public accountant (CPA), an individual must pass a series of examinations.[24] Once certified, the person must take an additional number of professional courses each year to maintain the license. Other professions such as human resources use voluntary professional certifications as standards of professionalism. These designations require specific education and experience.[25] The logic behind the use of designations is that discipline and standards of performance create a more competent, credible, and experienced professional.

For many jobs, competence is often determined by a second, less objective method for rating skill mastery. This happens as part of the annual performance-review process. The purpose is to characterize mastery as levels of performance expectations for any number of technical skills and nontechnical behaviors. For example, a manager might rate an employee's performance on a Likert scale such as

1 = fails to meet expectations;
2 = partially meets expectations;
3 = consistently meets expectations;
4 = meets and sometimes exceeds expectations;
5 = exceeds expectations.

Measuring competence only in terms of performance expectations, however, can be problematic. First, the fact that someone is rated as *meets expectations* doesn't necessarily mean the person has mastered a particular skill or competency. Is *meets* considered satisfactory, or should someone strive for *exceeds?* Second, expectations are not always explicit and clearly defined. Some managers meet routinely to set expectations; others set expectations once a year at the annual review. A third problem is the organizational inconsistency in defining and rating expectations. One manager's *exceeds* is another manager's *meets*. We're still left to question the levels of objectivity and consistency with which standards are used across the organization.

A different, more objective method for rating competence is the use of a continuum of skill mastery. Take the example of learning how to snow ski. The ratings might be

1 = learns the basics of balance, shifting weight, turning, and stopping;

2 = skis beginner trails and masters the basics;

3 = routinely skis the intermediate trails without falling;

4 = masters moguls and jumps;

5 = skis Suicide Hill and other expert trails with finesse.

The benefit of this approach is that it demonstrates a progression for how skill acquisition and mastery result in higher levels of performance. It also reflects a mindset and a culture for skill development. Rather than some generalized rating of meets or exceeds expectations, this approach incorporates the mastery of the skills needed to go from skiing the bunny slope to attacking Suicide Hill. It also means that the organization has taken the time to define standards and to encourage its members to continue to learn and strive to get better.

Mastery as an Intrinsic Motivator

Do you recall a high-school math problem about the possibility of walking out the doorway of a room if you take specific-size steps? From across the room you start with a full step, then a half-step, followed by half of that step, and so on. The question: Do you ever reach the doorway? The answer: Stay tuned.

Think of mastery as an element needed to build competence. *In Drive, the Surprising Truth about What Motivates Us,* Daniel Pink describes mastery in a context similar to the math problem. Mastery is something we continually strive for, to make it through the doorway. It is an important motivational force maximized by personal engagement rather than compliance to expectations or standards. Mastery is important not because it drives performing to a standard (an extrinsic motivator), but, because it pushes us to get better (an intrinsic motivator). As Pink puts it, "Mastery is the desire to get better and better at something that matters."[26]

According to Pink, there are three components to mastery:

1. "Mastery is an asymptote." In algebra, an asymptote is a straight line that a curve approaches but never touches.[27] Here is the high-school math problem revisited. Regardless of where you start in the room,

you never make it through the doorway—close, closer, closer, but never over the threshold. However, you are determined to get as close as you can. Such is the case with mastery. You get close, but never touch it. The motivation is continuous learning and improvement, the thrill of the chase, frustrating at times but nonetheless the drive that keeps you in relentless pursuit.

2. "Mastery is a mindset." According to psychologist, researcher, and author Carol Dweck, people tend to hold two different views of their intelligence: as an *entity*, meaning there is a finite amount of intelligence, or as *incremental*, meaning that, with effort, intelligence can be increased. Dweck explains that these two self-theories lead to different types of goals: performance goals and learning goals. When the goal is to perform, the focus is on results. When the goal is to learn, the focus is not just on results but what's learned from the experience. Learning keeps the mind fresh, active, and resilient. What is most telling between the two views is the difference in handling adversity. For the entity theory individual, the feeling is one of helplessness or failure when confronted by adversity. For the incremental theory individual, the feeling is one of mastery, because one can always strive to get better.[28] In the context of leadership development, mastery is about striving to get better.

3. Mastery is pain. In citing studies conducted on West Point cadets, Pink describes what separates those that make it through boot camp isn't physical stamina or athletic ability: it's grit. According to sociologist Daniel Chambliss in his study of Olympic swimmers, "grit may be as essential as talent to high accomplishment."[29] Geoff Colvin reaches a similar conclusion about "what really separates world-class performers from everybody else." It's deliberate practice, which psychologist Anders Ericsson describes as "not inherently enjoyable."[30] To say the least, mastery is handling the mundane with resilience and determination.

Expertise Is Getting Smart

Expertise is a potent combination of motivational energy, analytical judgment, basic curiosity, and skill mastery. It is much more than acquiring knowledge or logging time. Rather, it is a dynamic state where experimentation, learning, insight, and practice get you close to but never reach a state of mastery. It's fueled by the need to achieve and get results. It requires balancing discernment and curiosity—to stay grounded but nimble, logical but not too logical, confident but questioning. Expertise is critical to leadership but alone does not predict leadership success.

It's not about being smart, it's about getting smart.

Getting smart is going to be a theme throughout the leadership-development process. It starts with learning about the job. Next it turns to learning about people.

Chapter Summary

Mentoré leadership stage comparisons

Expertise stage
What
Track record
Knowledge & experience
Depth
Student of knowledge
Native intelligence
How smart you are
Knowing your subject matter

Taking Stock

- One theme in leadership development is understanding basic motivation. David McClelland's theory of motivation describes three sources of motivational energy we possess that influence the way we think and shape our behavior. Power is the motive of influence; achievement, the motive of goal attainment; and affiliation, the motive of close, personal connections.

- A second theme in leadership development is understanding of how we think and learn. Gardner uses the concept of multiple intelligence and minds to describe different perspectives and points of view. Argyris describes single- and double-loop learning, the difference between looking at actions and assumptions behind the actions. Pink describes differences in logical, analytical left-brain thinking and emotional, intuitive right-brain thinking. Leadership is going to take whole-brain thinking.

- The first stage of leadership development is expertise. Expertise is a platform supported by four basic competencies: initiative, discernment, curiosity, and competence. Together they create the base upon which other leadership skills, competencies, and behaviors are built.

- Initiative is intrinsic motivation. It is drive, the need to achieve. It is the fuel that converts thoughts into actions, and actions into results. Even beyond the stage of expertise, initiative is important as a willingness to jump in, step up, take responsibility, and get results.

- Discernment is the ability not only to think logically, but to form judgments. By stepping back and gaining perspective, discernment searches not only for causation but also for meaning and insight. Discernment moves from what to why. It helps sort through an avalanche of data to find what's most relevant. Moving forward, the ability to make informed judgments with less-than-perfect information will be integral to effective leadership.

- Curiosity is asking questions, particularly what if, and opening closed doors. Curiosity is not logical and it likes that by itself. Curiosity is inquisitiveness, sometimes unrestrained, and willing to take intellectual risks. While curiosity may not jump completely out of the box, it at least opens the lid and looks outside.

- Competence in specific terms is knowing when and how to apply knowledge and skill to a range of situations to get results. In general terms, it is knowing your stuff and doing a good job. Competence is fluency. It represents a perpetual state for learning, where the life of work and work of life are exciting and motivating.

- Thinking about thinking is the doorway to reflection and insight. These are particularly important as you move into the other stages of leadership development.
- Expertise is important as a base component of leadership. Expertise alone, however, does not guarantee leadership success.

What You Can Do Tomorrow

There are many activities and situations that you can engage in to build a base of expertise. In doing so, this is also a great way to engage others in the process—your manager, senior leaders in the organization, and your colleagues. It's all about getting smart, which makes this a continuous process. Given as follows is a list of activities for you to consider and to spark other ideas.

Ideas and Activities to Build Expertise

Take Initiative

- Tackle an important task that your organization has discussed but no one has taken on.
- Volunteer to work on a project with experienced individuals where you can learn something new.
- It's not unusual for individuals to complete a task at the 80 percent level, but finishing is another story. Make sure that you close out every important task in front of you. Think about who you need to inform once that it is complete.
- Taking initiative is an attitude, but it's also a drive to action. Initiative is taking steps in a desired direction. Write down your goals and objectives. Make them real, actionable, concrete, and measurable where you can.

Increase Discernment, Judgment, and Problem-Solving Capabilities

- Look for challenging assignments that test your reasoning and problem-solving ability.
- Find others who you think are good problem solvers. Spend time with them to understand not only what they do but how they think through a given situation.
- Enlist the help of a leader and potential mentor who is a good teacher, willing to share his or her ideas and impart knowledge as well as challenge and test your abilities.
- Read biographies or autobiographies of great leaders, particularly in your field of interest. Look for how they thought through and made judgments. What can you learn from them? Take notes and ask yourself what these ideas mean to you.

Stay Curious

- Think about new ways to solve the same situation or how to use the same solution to solve related problems.
- Look across situations and problems to see if there are patterns and explanations that are not obvious at first glance.
- Curiosity leads to creativity and innovation, and that happens in context by discussing ideas with others. So seek out colleagues to test ideas and assumptions. Buy them pizza if you need to bribe them.
- Don't jump at the first answer or explanation that you find. Don't be afraid to dig deeper or dig differently by asking what if.
- Curiosity fosters insight, and insight can strike when you least expect it. Don't be afraid to let your imagination kick in, even when your thoughts don't seem relevant. The *aha* moment can hit you in the shower or on the drive home. Don't miss out.
- Ask good questions. Perfect the art of probing to get below the surface level of a situation. Look for examples and specifics.

Build Competence

- Competence is skill mastery and proficiency. Think of it as a process, not an end state. This keeps you engaged, humble, and hungry for more knowledge.
- Ask for feedback from your manager, colleagues, or others whom you trust. It's not just performance feedback that's important, but it's also learning and getting ideas that lead to greater proficiency.
- Test your ideas and assumptions with colleagues. Learn from them.
- Learn from mistakes, both your own and of the team. Contribute to an environment of learning, not blaming. Carry over this same attitude when asking for feedback if something did not turn out the way you wanted. Think problem solving, not blame.
- Debrief all key decisions, initiatives, or projects. What did you learn? What changes, if any, are needed?

CHAPTER 3

Stage Two: Credibility

A Kaleidoscopic Shift

Life in the Labyrinth

Previously we discussed that building expertise answers the question what—What do I need to know and do to execute my role effectively? The value derived from technical expertise is the application of knowledge and experience to solve problems, get results, and create greater efficiency and effectiveness in the process.

In stage two of leadership development, the focus changes from expertise to credibility. Building credibility answers the question who—Who do I need to build relationships with in order to execute my role effectively? Credibility is the medium through which others trust you, and as we will see, this trust is built on your ability and desire to help others solve their problems.

Credibility and trust are the foundation for building relationships. While expertise can be measured objectively in terms of concrete metrics or standards of performance, credibility is measured subjectively by others' perceptions. It is not simply what you do, but how others perceive what you do that makes you credible.

How can you impact this perception? Demonstrating technical, job-related expertise is clearly part of the answer, but expertise alone does not make you credible. Credibility is not simply about how smart you are, your experience, or your title. In fact, it is not about you at all. It's about the other person. It's about your ability to connect with others and provide something of value to them. If expertise requires you to be a student of subject matter, then credibility requires you be a student of people.

Credibility

Credibility stage

Credibility is built on your ability to commit and deliver value to others. It is the basis for developing and managing relationships. It is an important stage for any new leader, and is also critical for the technical professional looking to achieve technical status as a subject matter expert.

Credibility competencies

Relationship management: establishing rapport, making connections, building relationships, and creating networks critical to both short- and long-term goals

Character and moral courage: the demonstration of integrity and the highest professional standards even when facing adversity or making the tough decisions—how you choose to do business

Credibility and trust: building a positive reputation based on your ability to commit and deliver value to others

Effective communication and influence skills: the ability to listen, to communicate at the level of the audience, and to persuade others effectively by identifying common ground and striving for mutually beneficial outcomes

If expertise is measured in terms of IQ or native intelligence, then credibility is measured in terms of EI or emotional intelligence.

Relationship Management as Emotional Intelligence

In 1995, Daniel Goleman changed the landscape of leadership development by introducing the concept of Emotional Intelligence.[1] Goleman followed in the footsteps of a now familiar name, David McClelland, Harvard professor and authority in the field of motivational research, and Goleman's main thesis advisor. Historically, McClelland emerged from a long line of 20th century researchers interested in performance excellence. In the early part of the century, Frederick Taylor described performance in terms of movement and efficiency, studying people as machines. Following Taylor was the introduction of IQ as a standard for performance. IQ equated success with mental capacity. Then Freudian thinking and personality factors began to play a role in characterizing performance.[2]

In the early 1970s, however, McClelland wanted to test for *competence* rather than IQ.[3] He and his research team began interviewing star performers in organizations to determine what they did and how they thought in a series of self-described critical events. What they discovered has ushered in the modern-day era of competencies as behavioral standards for performance—the knowledge, skills, traits, and pattern of habits that differentiate outstanding from average performance. Other McClelland colleagues including Boyatzis[4] and Spencer[5] dug deeper into an understanding of these competencies and derived a similar finding: interpersonal skills, not IQ, are better indicators and predictors of performance excellence. In quoting Spencer's findings, Zenger writes: "The competencies of achievement orientation, influence, and personal effectiveness will likely account for 80 to 98 percent of all competency models."[6]

Goleman's interest was in researching the brain to understand how logic—left-brain thinking—and emotion—right-brain thinking—interact to create successful performance. What Goleman has given us is the language to characterize a unique set of performance-enhancing behaviors. Simply stated, EI is the ability to connect with others. Goleman's research demonstrates that building these connections is not secondary, optional, or soft. It is primary, necessary, and hard for successful performance. And EI takes on an even larger role in characterizing leadership effectiveness.[7]

A Turn of the Kaleidoscope

Goleman tells us that EI begins with self-awareness and self-regulation. It starts with knowing what is critical and important to you, the individual.

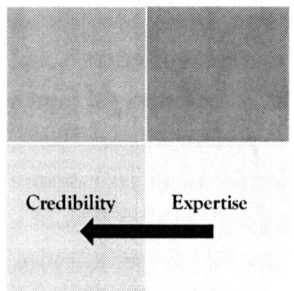

With this knowledge as a base, a person moves from self-knowledge to understanding what is important to others. Rapport, empathy, and what Goleman describes as social radar create this ability to connect.[8]

This insight is important because it marks the point of inflection from expertise to credibility, a point characterized as (a) a change in perspective—from me to others—and (b) a change in mindset, from technical expertise to personal credibility. However, this shift doesn't mean that technical expertise goes away. Rather, the shift is an evolution of understanding that personal effectiveness and job performance are part of a bigger equation. Like turning the kaleidoscope, the picture changes, and what you *see* changes as well. To build technical expertise, you *see* situations; to build credibility, you *see* people.

Empathy, Making an Emotional Connection

> *We are wired to connect.*
> Daniel Goleman

An emotional connection is connecting on a personal level, and this is a huge part of emotional intelligence. At the base of these connections is empathy, the ability to *recognize* the emotions in others. When empathy is real, there is heart-felt sincerity and a personal connection. When empathy is faked, the insincerity is palpable and destructive.

Emotional situations require the ability to tune in at an emotional level. Conger points out that using logical reasoning in emotional situations does not work. When logic and emotion collide, there is no connection.[9] When a person is emotional—angry, frustrated, or discouraged—using logic to convince that individual not to be angry, frustrated, or discouraged does not compute. For example, you go to the dealership to pick up your car from a routine service appointment. The manager tells you it won't be ready until tomorrow. You're angry (emotion). He tells you the part did not arrive, the mechanic went home early with the flu, and the dog ate your paperwork (all logical reasons). Now you're really angry (more emotion).

A better response in this situation is, "Dr. Doll, I know you're angry and you have every right to be. I said your car would be ready at 5pm and it isn't. Let me drive you home now and arrange to get you in the morning. If you'd prefer to take a loaner, I can have it ready to go in five minutes." What makes this response better is the connection—"I know you're angry and you have every right to be." Excuses are attempts at logical justifications. Better to work at an emotional level first, and then move forward.

Choosing How You Do Business

Character and Moral Courage

Character, while an important element in building credibility, is considered by many leadership experts as the most essential characteristic for leadership success. Character is what 19th century author Cyrus Bartol describes as "the diamond that scratches every other stone, the only source of power that can add or subtract from every other source."[10] Contemporary experts in the leadership field, Bennis,[11] Kouzes and Posner,[12] and Covey,[13] also describe the important role that character plays in effective leadership. Zenger and Folkman, whose research spanned more than 25,000 leaders, are emphatic: "Our research confirms that personal character is absolutely at the heart of effective leadership."[14]

Your image

Here is something for you to consider:

How do you describe your own image, meaning, how do you think you do business?

How do you think others describe your image?
Don't know? Ask two people whose opinions you value—they don't have to be your best friend or your sworn enemy.

Struck by the power of first impressions you have of other people? What's the first impression others have about you?

To what extent does how you see yourself and how others see you impact what you want to do as a leader?

Character defines the individual as culture defines the organization. Both represent a way for doing business. In contemporary speak, character is your personal brand. The way people judge how you do business is based on behavior, not words. We think of character as how a person constructs his own unique context, a personal culture created by his decisions, choices, and most importantly, actions.

Critical to character are integrity and professionalism, the standards to which a person adheres in everyday transactions and personal interactions. Character speaks to an appreciation of what makes us alike and a sensitivity and respect for what makes us different. Character is also moral courage, the confidence to make tough decisions and do what is right, even in the face of opposition. If technical competence is the head, and EI, the heart, then character is the soul.

Trust-Building Behaviors

Build a Track Record of Success

One of the first opportunities to build credibility begins by using technical expertise to build a track record of success. This is a conscious process, not simply a secondary gain for doing good work. Even in the swirl of daily activity, a person can choose to build a track record and reputation as someone capable, competent, consistent, and reliable. It is the self-awareness that, as you gain experience, there are many opportunities to provide value to others. When people see you working in their best interests and helping them solve their problems, they remember. Small actions like a timely response to an e-mail, following up after a problem is resolved, or just checking in with a colleague make big differences. Conversely, when others feel ignored or dismissed by a lack of response, personal credibility is diminished.

From the Cube to the Hallway

First popularized by management guru Tom Peters, the concept of "Management by Walking Around"—MBWA—affirms the importance of visibility, the need for a manager to be out and about.[15] Visibility builds credibility. Like Peters, I had the opportunity to work with several people at Hewlett-Packard who told the legendary stories of the company's founders, how they made the rounds when visiting an H-P facility, talking to different individuals or working with a project team, eating pizza, and staying until late at night to lend assistance.

The need for visibility, however, is not limited to managers. Given the complexity of modern-day organizations, visibility can be challenging and time consuming for anyone. Therefore, there is value for you to leave the cube and hit the hallway. Think of it as "Credibility by Walking Around"—"CBWA." Since visibility and direct communication are at a premium, taking a proactive step to be out and about increases personal accessibility, two-way communication and dialogue, and ultimately credibility and trust.

Strategic Visibility

Get in Front of the Right People

Another credibility-related consideration is increasing visibility to senior management both inside and outside your organization. One opportunity

---

Visibility

Think about increasing your visibility and credibility with specific people. For example:

Look through your calendar for the next two weeks. Identify a person with whom you need to spend time because he is a key person but you don't interact with him routinely. Make sure that you are visible at the meeting by spending a few minutes one on one, and setting up a time to meet to discuss something relevant to both of you.

Is there a particular senior-level manager, either in your organization or in a different group that would be beneficial to get to know? Work with your manager to determine how you might get in front of this individual. This could be making an introduction, asking you to be present at a meeting, or setting up a lunch together. Meeting with them can often take the form of drawing on their experience and insight into a particular issue and to share your perspective as well.

is to join a cross-functional initiative. Often these projects enable you to meet key individuals in other organizations and expand your networks. Depending on the nature of the initiative, you may also have direct access to senior leaders across the organization. A second and longer-term consideration is to strategize with your manager about what leaders in what organizations you need to get in front of as part of your professional development.

Build Networks

Networks constitute unique sets of relationships. One type of network consists of those individuals in the critical path of accomplishing a goal. Your interactions with them is through a network of relationships created for a particular purpose such as completing a project, implementing a program, or securing resources. How you maintain these connections afterward is critical.

Another type of network has less to do with a particular goal and more to do with building a broad base of support. You join a cross-functional task force because it gives you access to individuals and senior leadership in other departments that you might never meet on your own. You join professional organizations to exchange war stories and best practices, perhaps to look for a job or search for a job candidate. You join the board of the Boys and Girls Club to meet important community leaders. As Uzzi and Dunlap describe, these types of connections broaden your base of credibility and influence through access to information and people with different skill sets and different networks.[16]

Visibility Without Physical Presence

Step Up One-on-One Communications

Working face-to-face with people has the advantage of physical presence, direct observation, and the opportunity to read nonverbal cues. What is more challenging is visibility without physical presence—working with virtual teams, or business partners in different locations, or customers and suppliers anywhere in the world. Teleconferences and virtual meetings do not have the same impact as face-to-face interactions. What is critical for creating effective working relationships in these situations is to build visibility outside of these meetings through one-on-one communications.

People in procurement, for example, understand the importance of talking to their suppliers on a routine basis, many of whom they have never met face-to-face. They do not rely on e-mails or teleconferences to substitute for a more personalized, higher touch, and visible presence. Take the example of a successful project manager who has a worldwide implementation team. Not only does she speak with key individuals in advance of critical meetings, she follows up with personalized discussions—not e-mail—as needed. She understands the need to be visible even when physical presence is not possible. Furthermore, she knows that when she does travel to certain locations, she makes a point to meet project team members and build rapport in less-formal settings. It is amazing what sharing a coffee or having an adult beverage after work can do when meeting individuals with whom you normally have long-distance relationships.

The bottom line: when you are out of sight, consider yourself out of mind. Do not rely on group meetings to substitute for more personalized, one-on-one communications when you need to establish visibility and presence.

Connecting at a Personal and Emotional Level

Activity

Making personal and emotional connections is more than saying, "I feel your pain." If you were to say that, do not be surprised if someone retorts, "You have no idea how I feel." Connecting is at a person to person level—me and you. It takes several forms:

1. Listen closely to others when they are talking about something important and potentially emotional, and think about how best to respond. Especially, if someone wants you to listen or begins talking out a situation, the best thing for you to do is listen and speak judiciously. Making a connection means acknowledging the emotion, such as saying "that's tough, you have every right to be angry," "you

have to feel good about this," or "how are you holding up" are acknowledgments at a personal, emotional level. You don't have to overdo this. Be real and sincere.

2. Use the power of a personal note, as in an old-fashioned written note. The 5 minutes it takes to write demonstrates personal sincerity and attention. A written thank you note or a card to colleagues or team members speaks volumes. E-mail for this purpose is a distant second.

3. Check in with colleagues, associates, direct reports, even your manager, with no agenda other than to see how someone is doing. In-person is better than the phone, but both work.

4. Think of someone who you think easily connects with others, people with different interests and backgrounds. Observe what they do and how they do it. If you know them well, ask them about what they're thinking and doing in making connections.

5. Watch for situations where someone misses an opportunity to make an emotional connection. Perhaps, they respond with logic and reason to a situation where someone is frustrated. Observe the response. Make a mental note of what you would do differently in that situation.

6. You don't have to sound like Dr. Phil or Oprah to make emotional connections. Be respectful of others, and be yourself. This is a conversation that needs to be in your own voice.

7. Use a journal or diary to make weekly notations for one meeting or interaction in which you felt you connected well with an individual or group on a personal level. Recall what you thought, said, and did that created the connection. Think of a situation or interaction that did not go the way you wanted it to go. What was missing? What would you do differently?

8. Connecting and networking with people you don't know is sometimes difficult. Prepare for the next networking situation in which you're involved, such as a professional association or perhaps a meeting with people in another department you don't know that well. The key is rapport, looking for something in common with others. Think of three to four questions that you can ask that would open the door to a conversation. (Here's a big hint—last year's insane

winter weather, the Red Sox, the latest phone app, or the trials of raising teenagers.)

Effective Communication

You might think that a leader must have good communication skills as a prerequisite for getting the job. This is like saying that a bartender must know basic drink recipes in order to get hired. However, Zenger and Folkman tell us that effective communication is actually at a premium for leaders. It's not something that every leader possesses; rather, it differentiates outstanding from average performers. One of the unique distinctions is that effective leaders routinely rely on two-way communication to encourage input and buy-in.[17]

Drucker also weighs in on the importance of communication. He describes how the amount of communication in contemporary times would be unimaginable to those who first began to study the problems of communication in organizations. Drucker laments:

> Communications have proven as elusive as the unicorn. The noise level has gone up so fast that no one can really listen anymore to all the babble about communications. But there is clearly less and less communicating.[18]

And Drucker wrote this in 1974!

In chronicling the fundamentals of effective communication, Drucker stresses the ability to listen. He uses Plato's analogy that one must "speak to carpenters in carpenter metaphors" to emphasize understanding your audience. And, he stresses the importance of communication in the conveyance of perceptions, expectations, demands, and information.[19]

The Crucible: The Conversation

It is difficult to think of a skill today that could be any more important than effective communication. The crucible—the place where communication is maximized, where two people together can transform thoughts and feelings into decisive and responsible actions—is through one important structure. That structure is *the conversation*. Conversations are critical dialogues where there is both speaking *and* listening. By intent, conversations engage. Drucker says it best: "There can be no communication if it is conceived as going from the 'I' to the 'Thou.' Communication works only from one member of 'us' to another."[20]

Here's the operative thought: "from one member of us to another." Recently, a colleague expressed frustration at a meeting of the firm's leadership where they discussed a new project. Apparently, there was open communication, the part about saying what's on your mind and putting agendas on the table. But what was missing was engagement. My colleague's assessment of the problem: no one listens. Talking without listening is a monologue, and dueling monologues do not equal a dialogue, much less a conversation.

> *Talking without listening is a monologue, and dueling monologues do not equal a dialogue, much less a conversation.*

Active Listening

Most of us understand the speaking part of communication. To build credibility, however, the part to master is listening, specifically active listening.

Active listening incorporates the following elements that I describe as the *FLÉR* principle:[21]

1. Focus

   Whether in one-on-one or group discussions, face-to-face or telephone conversations, active listening begins by focusing on the individual who is speaking. In face-to-face interactions, focus requires direct eye contact and open posture. Telephone discussions require listening. Think of this as uni-tasking, not multitasking, such as talking to one person and e-mailing another person simultaneously. Whether sitting around a table at a meeting, eating lunch, or sitting behind your desk, to *engage* in conversation, focus on the other person. Ditch the distractions. And most importantly, clear your head. Be prepared to listen.

   Several years ago, I had a client who described a situation where he needed to discuss a very sensitive and immediate personal issue.

He was extremely upset, so he called his manager and said he really needed to talk. Because it was very quiet on the other end of the call, he thought his manager was really listening to what he had to say—until he heard tapping on the keyboard in the background. When someone says "I need to talk," take that as code for "I need you to listen." Multitasking is not the focus in this case; it's disrespect.

2. Listen

Listening is disciplined. It is the ability to be present, in the moment, with a stilled and focused mind. Listening is also facile and spontaneous. It is the ability to hear beyond the spoken word. It takes practice, lots of practice. Daniel Pink makes a relevant point. Pink says, that "we are our stories."[22] If that's true, then conversations are stories within the story. As the listener, your role is to understand the other person's story—the characters, the plot, and the big so-what moment. If the other person is not telling a story, your role is to help him or her by asking questions and getting the appropriate details.

Listening also requires the ability to ask probing questions at the appropriate moment. If you need detail, clarification, or information, asking who, what, and when is important. If you need to understand more subjective, evaluative information such as the person's perspective, motivation, or perception, asking *open-ended questions* such as how and why is appropriate: "How did others react to Avi's response?" "Why did you decide not to speak up?" "What do you think Sonja was thinking? Why were you upset about what she said?"

Open-ended, probing questions are one of the more critical communication skills, and they directly link to active listening. Sometimes people feel that asking questions is unnecessary or rude. However, asking questions appropriately serves three purposes:

- Asking questions is a way to understand not only the facts but what someone is thinking or feeling during a situation. Most of us tend to talk at a surface level, like "the meeting was a disaster" or "you know how Charlie is," or—my personal favorite—that something was "interesting." Without probing, how will you know why this person thought the meeting was a *disaster*, what makes Charlie *Charlie*, or what *interesting* means in this case. There's more to be understood, and effective probing is one way to get below the surface.

• Asking questions is a way to keep the conversation on track. Some individuals want to discuss all the details, or jump from one topic to another. An appropriate question like, "can you give me a headline here" or "what's the bottom line," or "what was the next most important part" are techniques to keep the conversation headed in the right direction.

• Asking questions is an indication of interest and concern, meaning that you want to understand what's critical to the person who's speaking. If your questions are fast and accusatory, the person may feel that he or she is under investigation. But when your questions are open and reaffirming, the person can sense a personal connection.

3. Engage[23]

Engagement is the give and take of the conversation, an acknowledgment of what's important from both a logical and emotional perspective, and an opportunity to move the conversation forward by taking action when appropriate. If there is a need to resolve a problem, engage in discussing next steps. If there is a need to align expectations, engage in how you will do that. When people are engaged in true dialogue, it builds what Covey describes as the "emotional bank account," the currency for building trust and, as we will see, effective leadership.[24]

4. Restate

Restatement or paraphrasing is the act of playing back what you've just heard. It serves two purposes: It demonstrates that you are listening, and it is an opportunity to see if you get the story right. When you restate by saying something like, "Let me see if I understand what you're saying," you let the speaker know that you *value* what she has to say. Like probing questions, restatement is a powerful communication and credibility-building technique.

"Speaking to Carpenters With Carpenter Metaphors"

In building credibility, the pendulum swings from understanding the *job* to understanding the *people* with whom you are working. Most of us operate as if the world thinks like we do. With building credibility, however, comes this insight: It's not about you. It's about the people with whom you interact. Where this is particularly important is when it comes to speaking the language of your audience.

Have you ever witnessed a meeting that blew up because someone delivered a highly technical presentation to a group of people that didn't understand one thing about what was being said? In this situation, it's the presenter who missed it. The assumption that the audience shares the same level of knowledge, need for detail, or even general interest is flawed. Tailoring the message to the individual or group with whom you are communicating is mandatory for credibility. It entails advanced preparation and on-the-spot adjustments: the EI needed to understand and read an audience. When successful, matching your communication to the audience creates acceptance. Failure to match the level of understanding creates all types of questions that can lead to mistrust. Because perception drives credibility, you have to learn to speak the language of the people with whom you're dealing, not the other way around. Without a common base of understanding, there's little traction for building credibility.

Understanding the Perspective of Others

Understanding the perspective of others is the extent to which you can articulate what is critical to another person, walk in their shoes, and view the world as they do. It is the expression of your appreciation for the other person's point of view. When people feel that you have heard them, that you understand their perspective, they are more likely to trust you. Understanding another person's perspective, however, does not mean that you necessarily agree with it. What it signifies is that you are listening and understand their viewpoint. As we shall see, understanding what is important to others is the starting point for another important credibility-building behavior, influence.

Effective Influence

Influence is derived from the power motive that McClelland describes, the need to have a desired impact on others. Influencing others happens through the power of building relationships. Bacon notes that it should come as no surprise that "we say yes to the requests of someone we know and like."[25] Bacon tells us that interpersonal relationships are based on reciprocity, a mutual exchange of give and take.[26] What this means is that if I cooperate with you, I expect you to cooperate with me. This give-and-take framework inside relationships is where cooperation, collaboration, influence, commitment, and buy-in take place.

Just how important is influence to job success? Although he started with a somewhat different premise, Daniel Pink wanted to find out. Beginning with an analysis of his own calendar and later commissioning a study he dubbed the "What Do You Do at Work Survey," Pink reached two major conclusions from the surveys of more than 7,000 adult full-time workers in the United States:

1. People are spending more than 40 percent of their time at work engaged in nonsales selling—persuading, influencing, and convincing others in ways that don't involve anyone making a purchase. Across a range of professions, we are devoting roughly 24 minutes of every hour to moving others.
2. People consider this aspect of their work crucial to their professional success—even in excess of the considerable amount of time they devote to it.[27]

This nonsales selling, what Pink describes as moving, is growing in importance, particularly as more people move into their own entrepreneurial businesses.[28] The need underscores my premise that leadership, the ability to influence others to the point they take decisive and responsible action, is a skill set that extends far beyond the traditional notion of managing others.

Influence Skills

Cialdini,[29] Bacon,[30] and Goleman[31] have identified several critical influence techniques and behaviors through their research. In consideration of their works and what I have found most effective in working with my clients, I break influence into four components:

1. Reading people—particularly to understand body language and nonverbal communication
2. Reading situations—to understand the politics, who has the power, who makes decisions, and how decisions are made
3. Role perspective—knowing what is important to others, to see a situation as they see it, to establish rapport and connect
4. Persuasion techniques—using techniques that are appropriate to the individuals and the situation

Each of these areas represents behaviors that someone can learn. Particularly for the uninitiated, effective influence requires increasing one's powers of observation, tuning in to people and situations, and following a skill-development regime that requires practice, patience, and feedback.

1. Reading people is fundamental for effective influence. For some, reading people is a sixth sense. It naturally informs. It has the quality of emotional intelligence that Goleman describes as social radar.[32] For others, reading people seems mystical, a clueless condition that my former business partner referred to as "a missing chip." In between these extremes lie the trainable skill of reading people from their verbal and nonverbal language, and the linkage, or disconnect, between the two. Dr. Albert Mehrabian claims that only 7 percent of any message is conveyed through words, while 38 percent comes through tone of voice, and 55 percent through nonverbal actions such as body language, facial expressions, and gestures. While some question these exact percentages, most agree that a significant part of communication is nonverbal and therefore important to understand the person and the real message.[33]
2. Reading situations is a bit trickier. Interpersonal dynamics and politics are critical. Understanding what's going on requires a keen sense of observation, watching how people interact and react to each other. Politics are linked to how decisions are made and who makes them. Understanding "who has the power" or "who calls the shots" is not always

obvious or based on the organizational hierarchy. Why is this important to understand? Imagine that you need sell an idea or influence the outcome of a decision. According to Pink, there is a 40 percent chance you could be doing this at any time on any day of the week. Here the mission is very clear: Find out how decisions are made, who makes them, and what you need to do to influence this person or group.

3. Earlier I described that understanding the perspective of others is important to build credibility. More to the point, it is fundamental for effective influence. Influence starts with understanding what is important to the person or people with whom you are engaged. It defines an area bounded by what others need and what you need, and it looks for common ground. As Goleman explains, it's also the basis for establishing rapport and the doorway to empathy.[34] Empathy springs from the affiliation motive that McClelland describes. It underlies meaningful relationships, and it is the currency of social interactions, the give and take of engagement that was described earlier. When we relate to each other, we understand each other. Agreement is not the point, but understanding is. Without the ability to understand others' perspectives, it is easy to launch into one-way, take it or leave it, selling mode. To quote Covey's Habit #5: "Seek first to understand, then to be understood."[35]

4. Using persuasion techniques, like communication in general, means understanding the audience and situation in which you are involved. Effective persuasion runs the gamut from the logical to the emotional. On the one hand, certain techniques are linked to logic, data, and understanding. They aim at the head. These techniques are commonly used as proof for why something should or should not happen. Particularly in technical environments, logical persuasion techniques reign supreme. On the other hand, there are techniques that appeal to emotion. They are linked to feelings and personal connections. They aim at the heart. "We're all in this together" and "doing what's right for the customer" are appeals to emotion, to create a common vision. When are these emotional appeal techniques effective? Conger describes this in "The Art of Persuasion."[36] When the situation calls for a personal connection ("You have reason to be

upset that your car's not ready"), emotional persuasion, not logical persuasion, is required. If you have any doubts, try using logic reasoning when someone is visibly emotional. To reinforce a general theme, the important point is your ability to match the techniques appropriately to the people and situations.

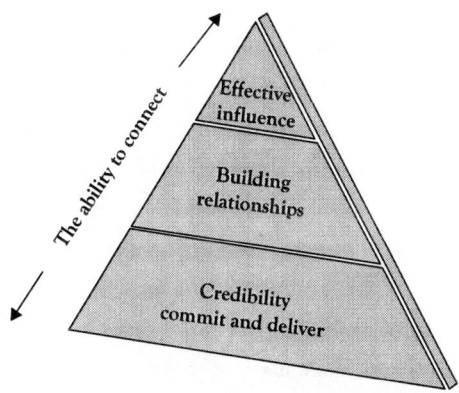

The Bottom Line: Commit and Deliver

Clients often ask me for a shortcut to build credibility. I have yet to find one. There is, however, one important practice that accelerates the credibility-building process. That practice is to find opportunities to *commit and deliver* something of value to someone else. This happens in one of two ways. One is when someone asks you for something directly—help in tracking down some statistics, handling a customer issue, or updating the team. The second is more strategic. In thinking about an individual or organization with whom you need to build credibility—such as a colleague, a new manager, or a business partner in another organization—you *proactively* find something of value to commit and deliver to that individual. For example, imagine you are working with another department to implement a new software package. Even though you meet biweekly with one manager, he mentions that he is frequently asked by his department head for a weekly update. You let him know that you want to help him, then meet offline to spec out what he needs, and create a spreadsheet that can be routinely updated. You found something of value, you committed, and then you delivered.

Why Is it Important to Commit?

I have worked with many clients who feel that doing a good job is who they are, what they do, and what is expected. Is there really a need to commit in some public way, and isn't this just some sort of psychological trick? Yes, absolutely, and no, not at all. To commit is to make a promise about what you will do. It is your word, plain and simple. It is clean, decisive. First the commitment, then the delivery. To commit and deliver is not about capability, bandwidth, or priority. It is a choice for how you do business. It is the demonstration of both your word and your actions, and this is what others value and remember about you.

What if you can't commit and deliver? Say so. Here is where the power of active listening and emotional connection also pay dividends. Let the other party know that you understand the request or issue (active listening), and that you acknowledge the importance or emotion behind it (emotional connection). Then state what you can and cannot do. Leveling with others is important. They may not like it, but they know that you've listened and given consideration to their request.

Barriers to Building Credibility

Moving from expertise to credibility is more about shifting gears than it is about trying to go faster, to accomplish more, or to be smarter. Some people, however, if left to their own instincts, face one of several barriers to building a base of credibility.

Barrier #1: The Lure of Technical Depth

Not everyone understands or appreciates the need to build a base of credibility and to connect with others. Many technical experts are high achievers, motivated by high standards and a need to get the job done right. From a motivational perspective, technical depth is a tremendous lure. It fuels the need for achievement. However, going for technical depth becomes problematic when an individual assumes that increasing expertise simultaneously increases credibility. The assumption that "*knowing more is worth more*" misses the point about how credibility is derived. It is not about how much you know or do that makes you credible. It is the value that others ascribe to what you know and do that moves the credibility meter.

Barrier #2: Smart, Arrogant, and Clueless

Can you think of someone you know who is technically brilliant but clueless when it comes to people? Problems arise, however, when an individual who is

> *A little knowledge is a dangerous thing. So is a lot.*
> Albert Einstein

technically competent makes assumptions about how important it is to be smart. When a person's motivation is to be right in every discussion, prepare for arrogance. When someone thinks he or she knows more and that makes him or her smarter, prepare for condescension and sarcasm. That can be damaging, dare I say, career limiting, when some of the less smart individuals on the other side of the discussion happen to be your senior managers.

Barrier #3: Speaking Up as "Kissing Up"

There are those who think that technical competence and doing a good job should speak for itself. Unfortunately, that's not always the case. To add a slight twist to an old adage, it's not what you know, it's who you know and how they attribute value to what you know that makes you credible. For some, this smacks of self-promotion. They feel that the whole idea of influence is political, dirty, a waste of time, and makes you nothing more than "a person who tries to get the approval of someone in authority by saying and doing helpful and friendly things that are not sincere."[37]

Speaking up about your knowledge or track record of success does not mean you have to "kiss up." Objectively discussing your accomplishments and how they have impacted others demonstrates self-confidence, pride, and even passion for your work. So the issue is not that a good job should speak for itself. The issue is that you want others to know that you appreciate what they need and value, and that you are or have been actively working to that end.

Barrier #4: Too Much Expertise, Not Enough Credibility

The Peter Principle 3.0

Technical expertise without credibility—native intelligence without emotional intelligence—only means that a person is smart, maybe even capable, but not necessarily valued. Where some people top out in their careers is at the point where they have demonstrated expertise but fail to launch in terms of credibility and relationship building.

This is variation of the Peter Principle first described in 1969 by Laurence Peter. Peter contends that people are promoted to their level of incompetence. Peter puts it another way: "the cream rises until it sours."[38] This suggests that something other than technical competence plays a role in successful career advancement. Daniel Goleman expresses a similar view. His variation of the Peter Principle: "too much college, too little kindergarten."[39]

As a corollary to the Peter Principle, a McClelland interpretation could be that people are promoted to a level where they no longer are capable of effectively influencing others. The achievement motive is the motive for doing good work. If people are promoted because they are the best based upon their achievements, eventually they reach a level in the organization that requires a different skill set, one based on the power motive. That skill set is influence, which we know is based on credibility, EI, and the ability to build relationships. Where technical experts get into trouble is when the achievement is at full throttle and influence is viewed as nothing more than drag. If you want to avoid advancing your career to the point of where you are incompetent, you may need to rethink your educational strategy: Say good-bye to college and hello to kindergarten.

A Subject Matter Expert, or Not a Subject Matter Expert, *When* Is the Question

Expertise is critical to success in any role, particularly in starting out in a career. For some people in roles, professions, or organizations that are technically based, the career path they desire is one of pursuing in-depth technical knowledge and experience. A point along this path is the designation and status of subject matter expert (SME). In professions such as information technology or engineering, the concept of an SME is closely associated with technical mastery or proficiency. Some professions might require tests, licenses, or certifications to achieve an SME status. Other organizations tag the designation of SME to a particular job level or position, such as a principal engineer. Professions such as medicine or law may not use the SME designation, but they apply a similar concept as a standard for specialization.

When is the point at which a person is considered an SME, and how much weight does technical expertise alone play in achieving that status? While it appears that the status as SME represents a standard of knowledge, proficiency, and experience, the need to bring value to others suggests the rites of passage for an SME status is actually through the credibility stage. It does not terminate with technical mastery.

In *The Extraordinary Leader*, Zenger and Folkman describe a link between interpersonal relationships and technical competence.[40] The authors cite groundbreaking research conducted at Bell Labs by Robert Kelley, the researcher who studied hundreds of scientists described as experts in their field.[41] They discovered the scientists who were most successful, were not the most knowledgeable, or had the highest IQs: "[What differentiated] these stars were that they performed their work differently. They developed strong networks within the organization and work with others in a totally different manner than the 'nonstars'."[42] The study also identified other interpersonal skills such as "helping colleagues solve problems and complete tasks, giving others credit, wanting to hear others' ideas, and working quietly without fanfare."[43] Furthermore, Kelley describes how the superstars embraced the need to tailor communication to the audience, confident in their knowledge without having to dazzle others with their brilliance. While Kelley did not call these individuals SMEs, he shed light on the relationship of technical competence and personal credibility in achieving recognition as experts.[44] The bottom line is that being considered an expert requires more than expertise. Even though some people may be called SMEs, their success is based on credibility-related competencies in addition to their knowledge and experience.

Like Expertise, Credibility Is Not an End-State

Relationship management, character and moral courage, trust, communication, and influence are essential competencies in the second stage of leadership development, the stage of credibility. Since credibility is in the eye of the beholder, it must be earned. The value attributed to you is based not just on what you know, but how you work with others. It is a personal shift in thinking, perspective, and behavior from the what to the who. For some, this is a major shift. It requires a different way of thinking about yourself and how you define success. It's not that expertise is unimportant, it's that another skill set is required.

Credibility requires two types of intelligence, intellectual and emotional. Credibility is built through a series of interactions that begin with a promise and end with delivering something of value to others, over and over and over again. While there is no formula per se, I submit if it takes x time to build credibility, it takes $0.01\ x$ of that time to destroy it. Credibility is not a given. It is not an end-state. It must be earned.

If moving into the credibility stage requires a shift, then moving into the next stage, alignment and execution, requires a leap.

Chapter Summary

Mentoré leadership stage comparisons

Expertise stage	Credibility stage
What	Who
Track record	Image & reputation
Knowledge & experience	Communication & influence
Depth	Breadth
Student of knowledge	Student of people
Native intelligence	Emotional intelligence
How smart you are	How you deliver value to others in the organization
Knowing your subject matter	Knowing your audience

Taking Stock

- The leadership stage of credibility represents a shift from competence and expertise to understanding people and building relationships.
- Daniel Goleman gives us the concept of EI to describe the competencies, skills, and behaviors needed to build personal connections and develop relationships that are critical to successful job performance, especially for leadership positions.
- Character and moral courage define how you do business with others. It's your personal brand and the image you project based on what's important to you and how you act and interact with others. Integrity, character, and moral courage enable you to "do the right thing."
- Building trust and credibility begin with creating a track record of success. The tipping point comes when you apply your knowledge and experience to others, to add value and help them succeed, solve their problems, and meet their challenges.
- Credibility is based on perception. The issue is not if other people get you, it's if you get other people. Understanding what's important to others is the starting point for building rapport, empathy, and effective relationships. If getting smart is the goal in the expertise stage, than getting smart about people is the goal in the credibility stage.
- Repeat this mantra to yourself: "Credibility is not about me, it's not about how smart I am, it's about the other person. Credibility is not about me . . ."
- Credibility is linked to follow-through, visibility, and communication. While there's no short cut for building credibility, your ability to commit and deliver on a continuous basis drives the process. Also, you need to be deliberately visible and accessible to the right people. Think "CBWA"—credibility by walking around. And, you need to tailor your communication to the individual or groups with whom you're involved.

- The conversation is the crucible in which credibility's work is accomplished. If you want to excel at one communication skill and one skill only, pick listening. Active listening uses the FLÉR principle: focus, listen, éngage, restate.
- Effective influence is based on trust and credibility. Influencing, what Pink calls moving, is currently what people at work (at least in the United States) engage in 40 percent of their day. That number is very likely on the rise. To a great extent, the elements of effective leadership are rooted in credibility, influence, and their associated skill sets. This one is not going away.
- The unique role of an SME, a subject matter expert, is not accomplished by simply building a base of expertise. It also requires building credibility, the skill set associated with the way in which you build relationships and use EI.
- Building a base of leadership, whether it's for a formal management position or just as likely a leadership position without formal authority, requires two critical skill sets. One is about getting smart. It's not about getting the right answer or performing at a certain level, it's about the process you take to get there—your ability to take initiative, engage the whole brain, and deliver results. The other skill set acknowledges that the right answers are only as good as your ability to understand the people with whom you interact and engage in the give and take of effective communication and influence. Expertise without credibility makes you smart. Expertise with credibility makes you smarter.
- Sarah Richman is back for more advice. What will you tell her about the need to build credibility, and how will you help her in the process?

Building Credibility and Emotional Intelligence

Ideas and Activities

1. Become a student of people. In particular, in meetings watch how people react in certain situations. Without passing judgment, why

do you think they did what they did? If it is someone you know, you may ask them after the meeting to tell you more about what they were thinking at that particular time.

2. Volunteer or be prepared to take part in resolving a problem or emotional situation with an internal or external customer.

3. If you are a new manager of a team or project with people with wide differences in experience and diverse backgrounds, think about meeting one-on-one to better understand each person's perspective. Have three to four good open-ended questions for discussion, such as what challenges do they see, or what's been their experience and insight in working through a particular type of project.

4. When you are involved in selling your ideas or getting commitment on a particular initiative, do your homework. Know who are the decision makers and get their perspective in one-on-one meetings or interactions in advance of the decision.

5. Build your own networks. Schedule at least an hour a week for sitting down with one or two people you need to know to expand your personal network inside or outside your organization. Dealing with bureaucracy at work? Build your own networks to help you get the answers and achieve results that you need.

6. Joining professional organizations is a great networking opportunity. Presenting at a conference where you are a member is even better. Joining a committee or volunteering for a leadership position is the best.

7. Ask a trusted colleague or your manager to give you feedback about your nonverbal communication, tone of voice, and body language during a key meeting. Particularly, if you've received feedback in the past that you come across as disengaged or emotional, you want to understand exactly what you do and how others perceive it.

8. When you find yourself getting upset or directly dealing with someone who you think is troublesome, make sure you create some emotional distance for yourself. Pause and think before you speak. Ask the other person to "tell you more" or restate what the person said as a way to calm the situation and yourself. Stay engaged but stay neutral. Know your hot buttons and what hooks you; be pre-

pared when you think you can't resist the bait. Losing your cool is not cool.

9. Pick one conversation a day to practice listening. Imagine that someone has a movie camera filming you at the time. Think about what you look like and sound like in that situation.

CHAPTER 4

Stage Three: Alignment and Execution

From Personal Competence to Organizational Capacity

Life in the Matrix

"Iacta Alea Est"

There Julius Caesar stood on the banks of the Rubicon River, January 10, 49 BC. In defiance of the ruler Pompeii, he knows that returning from Gaul with his army and crossing the Rubicon onto Italian soil amounts to treason. If he is to avoid a civil war, he must lay down his command, and surrender his troops and weapons. But if he and his troops cross the narrow bridge, there is no turning back. They will have entered Roman territory in a state of war. With a burst of energy Caesar declares, *"Iacta alea est"*—"*The die is cast.*" He and his troops march onward to Rome, and as they say, the rest is ancient Roman history.[1]

So there you stand at the bridge between credibility and alignment and execution. What got you to this point is a track record of success, a combination of your "technical chops," your ability to build relationships, and most importantly, your ability to deliver quality work that is valued by others.

Ahead of you is this vast territory known as "the business." Unlike Pompeii, the business implores you to cross the bridge, to help meet a bigger challenge, one where success is not measured by your personal accomplishment, but by your ability to impact the larger organization. The business presents you with different opportunities, but they all share one thing in common—the need to achieve results through others. Some of these opportunities are more traditional, such as people manager roles.

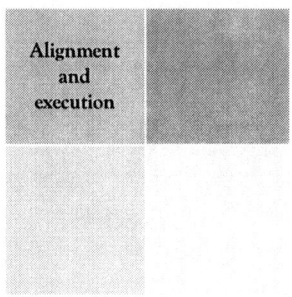

Alignment and execution stage

Alignment and execution is working through others to maximize performance and deliver results.

Alignment and execution competencies

Shapes the culture and political landscape: shapes a culture based on mutual respect, trust, and accountability

Builds an adaptive organization: creates a high-performance organization that gets results by continually aligning strategy, roles, skill sets, and leadership responsibilities

Develops talent: takes pride in role as coach and teacher who get the most out of individuals and teams

Leads by example: models the leadership behaviors and values expected of others

Others are new and different, like managing projects or leading ad hoc teams, heading up cross-functional implementation projects, or joining task forces. Such is life in the matrix. There is a greater emphasis on collaboration, to work with multiple reporting relationships across functional boundaries. Leading in these circumstances is often spontaneous and always dynamic. Potentially, every interaction and communication with people up, down, and across the organization is leadership-related, where your ability to influence others to the point they take decisive and responsible action is put to the test.

Personal competence got you to this point. Moving forward, personal competence alone is not going to be enough to maximize your impact.

The business needs you to achieve in a different way for a different purpose. And that purpose is to build organizational capacity.

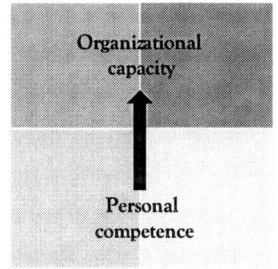

Moving into the stage of alignment and execution is not as easy as it appears. Individuals who have the knowledge, the track record, and the organizational respect *appear* ready to move beyond individual contributor roles into higher-level positions. For some, however, the transition is difficult. When given these opportunities to manage others, the momentum created by success as an individual contributor propels them to become a super individual contributor, an uber-achiever rather than delegate to others. It's what a client described to me as "adding more pluses," doing more because there's more to do instead of overseeing or handing-off work. However, the problem here is not just what they need to add or change. It's what they have to give up.

Give it Up, Step Up, Align, and Execute

Moving into alignment and execution answers the question how—*How do we achieve results?* This stage of development requires a uniquely different way of thinking and operating that changes where and how you spend your time. My experience in working with clients who have strong individual contributor backgrounds is that, left to their own instincts, they equate leading with having all the answers. This is a double whammy. First, thinking you need to have all the answers can lead to wanting—and getting—all the questions. Here is the scenario. People need answers. They form a line outside your door. There is a sign that says, "Take a number, and when I call it, be prepared to enter with your question." The question enters, and the answer exits. New questions will line up tomorrow. This process may confirm your importance, but it doesn't build organizational capacity. Second, as an uber-achiever, you create little impetus for others to build their personal competence if they can come to you to answer their questions. Have you trained them or have they trained you? Additionally, if people are *expected* to come to you for the answer, how motivating is that for those who want exciting and meaningful work, which is just about everyone?

To succeed in this stage, you have to give up thinking that your value is measured only by the depth of your expertise. Having answers is good; having all the answers, not so good. It may feel like you are losing ground if you do not continue to demonstrate your expertise, but you have a different role now. To expand your impact on the organization, the motivation you possess to get smarter and do great work should be directed at making others successful through the quality, delivery, and execution of *their* work. That is the job.

Some need to hold on tight, because you are about to give up control, control to do the job and to do it the way they would do it. As we will see later in the discussion of leadership style, this is a big struggle for high achievers. What has driven personal success are hands-on, high-quality results, but now your responsibility is to ensure that others execute successfully. Staying engaged is critical, but putting your hands on anything but a portion of the process is experienced by others as micromanagement. And now you are back to the "take a number" environment. What you give up is the need to be the best student even after you achieved "best student" status. What you need to achieve is

---

New Leader Activity

As a new leader, one of the biggest challenges is getting a handle of what you need to do more of, and what you need to do less of. This thought process never goes away.

In preparation for next week:

List one activity you need to do *less of.* Create a goal for what you will do by when.

List one activity you need to do *more of.* Create a goal.

Repeat this as part of your weekly scheduling for the next 12 weeks. At the end of that time period, take a close look at what you've accomplished. Review these observations with your manager and ask for feedback.

greater impact and influence on the organization. You have crossed the Rubicon. You have entered the matrix. Now your success and the organization's success are one and the same—increasing organizational capacity.

One of the most common concerns I get from clients today is that they need their leaders to step up and operate at a higher level. I think *they think* I know what that means, but I am never certain unless I ask. For the purposes of leadership development, I define stepping up and operating at a higher level as running the business, specifically, your piece of the business. Running the business is different from doing your job. It is literally a step up, not simply more of the same activity. In the alignment and execution stage, stepping up is understanding how things work and where you need to focus to have a favorable impact on the outcomes.

The Two Perspectives of Alignment and Execution

His name is Garrett Brown. He may not be a household name, but if you saw Rocky Balboa run up the stairs at the Philadelphia Art Museum, you can thank Mr. Brown for his invention of the Steadicam. But that is not all. With 50 patents under his belt, Mr. Brown created the Skycam, that great camera on wires that gives us the ability to see on-the-field action. The Skycam is now a staple for Sunday viewing of National Football League games. To see what New England quarterback Tom Brady sees with a little more height but from the same angle is stunning. We break from the huddle and go to the line of scrimmage. We look out over the defense, see the need for an adjustment, call an audible, and then execute the play. Sitting at home, watching from the safety of a flat screen television, we see 300-pound linemen engaged in hand-to-hand combat and 250-pound linebackers launched as human missiles as Brady finds his target for a first down. Thank you, Garret Brown, for allowing us to share an up close and personal Tom Brady experience from the comfort of our living room.[2]

This "*on-the-field view*" is one of two important perspectives needed in this stage of leadership development. This view focuses on *execution*. The minute the football is snapped each person has a job to do, to execute his or her assignments successfully. Then back to the huddle, call a new play, and execute again.

In addition, there is a coach who sits up in the press box. From this angle the coach has a higher, broader perspective that enables him to see patterns, identify strengths and weaknesses, and suggest changes. The *"press box view"* focuses on *alignment*, the extent to which all the parts work together to achieve successful execution. Afterward, as preparation for next week's game, the coaches and team study game films, digest observations, adjust the plays, and practice accordingly. Moving forward, both perspectives, "on-the-field" and "from the press box," are needed.

Alignment and Execution as Action Verbs

Alignment and execution is a unique blend of studying performance from different angles and focusing on how to create the conditions for successful outcomes. The competencies themselves represent four distinct areas for action:

1. *Shapes* the cultural and political landscape
2. *Builds* an adaptive organization
3. *Develops* talent
4. *Leads* by example

Shapes the Landscape

Like individual performance, organizational performance is defined by two critical dimensions: relationships, which translate into culture, and performance, which translates into operational efficiency for the business.

The Cultural-Relationship Dimension of the Landscape

Generally speaking, organizational effectiveness is dependent on the leader's ability to create the conditions for success within a defined context. This context is often referred to as the organizational culture. One of the first researchers in the field is Edward Schein, who defines culture formally as "a pattern of shared basic assumptions that a group learned as it solved its problems of external adaptation and integration ...."[3] Like Schein, Bolman and Deal were among the first to examine organizational culture, which they define simply "as the way we do things around here."[4] What Bolman and Deal contribute to the study of leadership is an understanding for the uniqueness of culture and the extent to which it shapes behavior. In particular, they ask three important questions:

- Are cultures definable entities?
- Do cultures contribute to measurable outcomes?
- To what extent does leadership play a role in shaping the culture?[5]

Culture as a Definable Entity

At one level, culture is impressionistic; it answers the questions, "What's it like to work here?" It's not unusual for someone walking into an organization for the first time to say they instantaneously get a "feel" for the place. Like the study of anthropology, the culture of an organization is the environment in which distinct values, beliefs, customs, rituals, and symbols mesh over time. Culture socializes people to the organization. Culture and acceptable behavior are self-reinforcing: They define each other. Culture is manifested in how people treat and engage with each other. If you want to "see" culture, look for three R's: what gets *recognized, rewarded, and reinforced.* Yes, cultures are definable entities.

The Culture—Outcomes—Leadership Connection

The relationship of culture, outcomes, and leadership is the key element in the seminal work of Jim Collins and team, *Good to Great.*[6] Collins identifies six specific elements of the culture and how they contribute to successful outcomes in good to great organizations:

1. The right type of leadership. Collins describes Level 5 leadership, a unique type of leadership that is a mix of personal humility and professional will.

2. The right team. The Collins summation that is widely quoted here is to "get the right people on the bus, the wrong people off the bus, and the right people in the right seats—and then they figured out where to drive it."[7] First who, then what.

3. A willingness to confront the brutal facts. Collins coins the concept of the "Stockdale paradox," named for the former prisoner of war who confronted the brutal facts of imprisonment but never lost faith that he would one day be freed.

4. The use of a *simplified* guiding principle that comes from a deep understanding of what you're best at, what drives your economic engine, and what you are deeply passionate about. Collins describes this as the "hedgehog concept."

5. A culture of discipline. Collins states, "All companies have a culture, some companies have discipline, but few companies have a culture of discipline . . . . When you combine a culture of discipline with an ethic of entrepreneurship, you get the magical alchemy of great performance."[8]

6. Technology accelerators. Technology is used not to ignite transformation, but to accelerate it.

Collins's analysis substantiates that leadership does impact culture, and that the cultural distinctions represented by good to great companies produce measurable, bottom-line results.[9]

Understanding the Culture and Political Landscape

The processes of decision making, communication, and problem resolution and prioritization have a significant impact on the culture and political landscape. Together they create a unique quality for how business is conducted both inside and outside the organization.

Decision Making

There are two components of decision making: the process for making decisions and the people who make them. Both inform the notion of "how we do things around here."

Consider the different options for making decisions:

- Top down through executive fiat
- Highly bureaucratic, where several sign-offs are needed before the decision is made
- Rationalized process in which a team frames the issue, collects data, considers options and trade-offs, and then makes an informed decision
- Highly participative or consensus building
- Is there a decision-making process at all?

Each option has cultural implications. Top-down decision making reinforces compliance. Bureaucratic decision making means dealing with red tape and time delays. A highly rationalized approach creates discipline. Being highly participative creates buy in, but it also can be time consuming. When there is no decision-making process, the situation is rudderless, where quasi- and non-decisions are "made" over and over again.

Then there are the decision makers. Their motivation, values, style, and most importantly, their behavior, set a political tone. The way in which they relate to others and make themselves available speaks volumes. In any given situation, these are the individuals whom you may need to influence to get buy in and commitment. How decision makers take counsel and invite participation set in motion certain patterns of behavior that contribute to what the culture looks like.

Communication

There are two aspects of communication that impact an organization's culture. One is the extent to which information is shared. When information is closely held, it creates a more political environment. Information is currency. The more someone has it, the more power they wield, and the more charged is the political climate. On the other hand, when information is shared, there's a greater sense of trust, transparency, and openness.

The other important aspect is how communication is structured. Bossidy and Charan describe these structures as "social operating mechanisms" that are used "anywhere that dialogue takes place." They emphasize that it is through these mechanisms that "beliefs and behaviors are practiced consistently and relentlessly."[10]

Types of communication structures and the questions that arise are:

- town hall, small group, and one-on-one meetings. Is the objective of these meetings clear? Are there agendas, or do people just wing it?
- voicemail and e-mail. These are good for conveying information but problematic for resolving problems. What is the purpose for each?
- collaboration rooms and hallway chit-chat. Is the communication planned or spontaneous?
- remote meetings. How do you maintain the right level of communication with colleagues whom you don't "see" on a routine basis, if ever?
- in-person communication. It still exists. How is it optimized?

Problem Solving and Prioritization

At a surface level, problem solving and prioritization may not look like they shape the culture, that is, until you look deeper. Like communication, problem solving runs the gamut. It happens on the fly, in routine meetings, or more methodically through a process for escalation. We know that problem solving is a fact of organizational life. It's how organizations approach problem solving—as reactive, anticipatory, or something in between—that defines the culture.

The same goes for prioritization. Consider these events ripped from today's business headlines: "Shipments delayed," "Customer changes mind," "The IT team defection continues," and "Winter storm closes down the East Coast." How an organization prioritizes and reprioritizes work is a process within the culture. *What does this process look like? How do people react? How are the changes communicated?* The extent to which an organization flexes and adapts, takes change in stride without losing momentum and focus, defines an important part of "what it's like to work here."

Culture and Its Impact on Climate

The culture of an organization also impacts the climate. Climate represents how people perceive the organization. In research associated with McClelland's concept of motivation, Spreier et al. describe six factors that contribute to workforce climate:[11]

1. Flexibility
   Flexibility is a measure of how employees perceive rules and policies. Are they dealing with red tape or helpful guidelines? To what extent are new ideas encouraged and accepted?
2. Responsibility
   Responsibility is critical because it defines *personal scope*. In one respect, responsibility defines personal autonomy, the latitude that someone has to perform his or her job. In another respect, responsibility defines an expectation for a deliverable, task, or process an individual is expected to perform.
3. Standards
   Standards are a set of clearly defined expectations that define a desired level of performance. Standards promote excellence when

---

Characterizing Your Organization's Culture

As a leader of a team, function, or organization, what are five adjectives that you think best describe the culture?

For a team activity, ask each team member to do the same. Be prepared to discuss the responses in an open and nonjudgmental forum. Think about similarities and differences in responses. How do these line up with your descriptions? What's the impact of these perceptions on the team's performance? Determine what three actions are needed moving forward.

For the trifecta, go to five people outside the organization whose perspectives you value. Ask them to describe what it's like to work with your group by using descriptive adjectives. How well do these impressions line up with your views and those of the team? What are the implications of these comparisons? What next steps are needed?

they are set at a high but attainable level. Standards represent what individuals are expected to accomplish to meet the organizational challenges.

4. Clarity

Clarity is organizational oxygen. It energizes. Clarity defines boundaries and delineates responsibilities. It connects individual responsibilities with organizational goals. Clarity creates expectations. It defines hand-offs and information requirements.

Lack of clarity is carbon monoxide. It kills. Sometimes the lack of clarity overwhelms and grinds organizations to a halt. More often, it is insidious. When decisions aren't made, objectives and outcomes aren't defined, or responsibilities aren't clear, there's activity, but not efficient and effective execution. According to Spreier, in study after study, clarity is the one dimension of climate that has the strongest link to productivity.[12] Stated another way, clarity creates effective organizational alignment, which in turn creates more effective execution.

5. Rewards

While compensation and formal recognition are important, the type of reward that is most desired is ongoing, objective feedback and recognition for a job well done.

6. Team commitment

When people are engaged, team commitment is high. People take pride in their work and are appreciated for their accomplishments. Commitment and engagement are a measure of the extent to which the other climate dimensions mesh together effectively.

Changing the Culture

Today it is popular to describe the need for changing the culture. Culture is often characterized in broad strokes, such as a customer-focused culture, or a culture of accountability or innovation. The simplification serves a purpose, which is to articulate a guiding principle about what is important. For cultural change to succeed, however, what's important or desired must be defined in behavioral terms. Changing the culture, particularly in the early stages, is more about changing behavior than it is changing the way people think. It's also important to align tasks, responsibilities, and processes to the outcomes the culture is intended to produce. We know that simply espousing what values are important does not mean that people will demonstrate them. Saying that teamwork is important only changes the culture if people actually *experience* effective teamwork and treat each other as team members. Cultural change is not easy, especially as economic conditions change and organizations scramble to adjust. As we'll soon discover, leading change of any magnitude, which includes a change in culture, requires a mindful, strategic process.

The Business-Operational Dimension of the Landscape

The High-Performance Organization

From the cultural-relationship dimension we move to the second dimension of organizational performance, which is business-operational. One method for analyzing business and operational alignment is the use of a high-performance organizational model. The concept of the high-performance organization is based on the principles of systems thinking. Systems thinking has its roots in the field of systems dynamics that began with MIT professor Jay Forrester in the mid-1950s.[13] Forrester applied the concepts used in engineering to explain the dynamics that exist inside social systems. The advantage of systems thinking is that it's possible to understand complex problems in terms of dynamics and interdependencies. Peter Senge, another expert in this arena, emphasizes that systems thinking, not simply cause–effect analysis, is needed to understand the impact of actions, patterns of behavior, and intended or unintended consequences on overall performance.[14] The value of systems thinking is that it looks at multiple relationships with the understanding that a change in one element impacts changes to other elements, and subsequently changes the overall performance of the system itself.

Using the high-performance organization model starts with drawing a boundary to define the system. Where the boundary is drawn is important. This could be at the team, function, department, or business level. The boundary delineates what is on the inside and within the control of the system, and what is external or exogenous, outside the control of the system but can impact system performance. From a business perspective, for example, external variables could include a new competitive threat, the loss of a major customer, new changes in the law, or a sudden change in the economy. These external forces are highly dynamic. While none falls within the business, they can impact how the business as a system performs. To accommodate the impact of these forces a system may need to realign or make major adjustments.

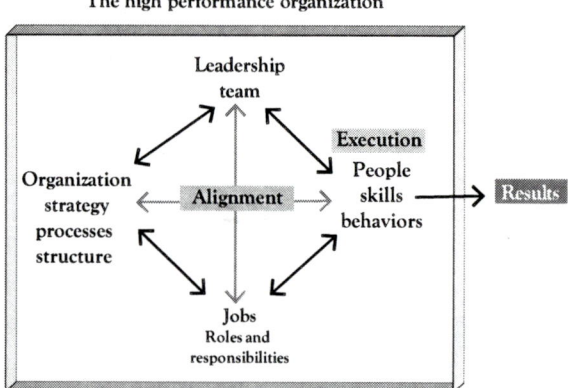

The high performance organization

The Four Elements of the High-Performance Organization

1. Leadership

   The element of leadership refers to the team of individuals accountable for long-term strategic direction, midterm alignment, and short-term execution. Operationally, leadership is the gyroscope needed to keep the organization on track. This requires simultaneously looking in two directions:

   • Outside the system, to constantly monitor the exogenous factors and their potential impact on the organization
   • Inside, to monitor quality and performance, to realign and adjust as required

2. Organization

   There are three critical components within the organizational element: strategy, process, and structure. Strategy is the high-level directional plan, the filter through which critical decisions must pass. Strategy determines what the organization will and will not do. Second are the critical business processes that are based on the strategy. The leadership team has the accountability to see that these processes run smoothly, to make improvements, or to reconfigure them when needed.

The third component is structure. In theory, structure is built upon critical business processes (as opposed to the other way around) to ensure process continuity across roles and functions. Other key considerations for organizational structure are

- work specialization, the degree to which activities are subdivided into separate jobs;
- departmentalization, how jobs are grouped;
- chain of command, the structure of reporting relationships;
- span of control, the number of individuals a leader can effectively direct;
- centralization or recentralization, the place where decision-making authority resides;
- formalization, the extent to which employees need prescribed policies and procedures.[15]

Today, more complex structures like matrix organizations and dual reporting relationships reflect the need for speed and agility. The benefit is one of improved cycle time through better hand-offs, better communication, and quicker response time.

3. Jobs

With strategy, process, and structure in place, the next element is to carve out roles and responsibilities. The use of the job wheel described in Chapter 2 is one method to determine responsibilities first, by looking at the position, and then identifying key interfaces (people or departments) and critical tasks that are associated with each.

Another method is the use of RACI charts, a technique widely used in the field of project management.[16] RACI charts use processes and the associated steps to make one of four assignments:

- R = responsible. *Who does the step?*
- A = accountable. *Who is accountable for the outcome, the completion of the step?*

- C = consulted. *Who needs to be consulted in the execution of this step, meaning whose input is needed?*
- I = informed. *As part of the communication process, who needs to be informed that this particular step is completed?*

Both the job wheel and RACI charts are appropriate tools to help with issues about roles and responsibilities. One of the biggest issues I experience in working with clients is the ongoing need for job clarity. The need exists at

- the macrolevel: generally, *what am I responsible for, what does success look like, and how will I be measured?*
- the microlevel: in a particular initiative, *who is responsible for what in this situation?*

> *Accountability designates ownership for the outcome. When an individual is accountable, he owns the outcome whether it is through direct hands-on activity or working through others.*

Another point of confusion is the difference between responsibility and accountability. I find that these are often used interchangeably when, instead, they should make clear differentiations. Responsibility refers to the specific duties an individual is expected to perform. Accountability designates *ownership for the outcome*. When an individual is accountable, he owns the outcome whether it is through direct hands-on activity or working through others.

As I mentioned earlier, the lack of clarity, particularly job clarity, is like carbon monoxide—you can't see it or smell it, and by the time it takes hold, it's too late. More often what the lack of clarity creates is a loss in productivity mixed with confusion and frustration, opportunity costs that can't be recouped.

4. People

Work is accomplished through people, not processes, equipment, or technology. From an organizational effectiveness perspective, what's important is to determine if people have the right skills and competencies to perform their jobs effectively. One method for identifying and assessing these is the job standards process discussed in Chapter 2. By first identifying duties and tasks, it's possible to define the technical or content-related skills and the critical competencies and behaviors needed for outstanding performance. In turn, the organization uses the skills and behaviors as a blueprint to select, assess, and develop employees.

The Relationship of Alignment to Effective Execution

The high-performance model is a framework for diagnosing organizational alignment. At a basic level, the model identifies how the elements align with each other. For example:

- *How well do roles align with the business processes?*
- *Are responsibilities and accountabilities assigned for each of the key process steps?*
- *What is the extent to which people in specific roles have the right skill sets?*
- *How smooth are hand-offs and the information flow across functions?*

At a higher level, the model detects how the overall system accommodates to a major change from either external or internal forces. For example, what happens to the system, the business enterprise, when there is a major economic downturn like the one we saw in 2008? The external change produces a change in strategy, which impacts the structure of the organization, which changes the nature of certain jobs, which in turn could require different skill sets. In this case, the external driver sets in motion a series of internal actions and reactions, sometimes planned, sometimes unintended. Sometimes the changes begin internally, such as the implementation of a new accounting system. A change in the process produces a change in how jobs are structured, which ultimately could improve productivity, reduce costs, and increase margins. Consider another example, like the promotion of a new division head. She comes to the job with a different strategic vision for the organization, signaling structural changes and putting "different people on the bus," all intended to move the business into new territory.

The role of the leader in alignment and execution requires constant vigilance of both relationship-cultural and business-operational issues. This takes an on-the-field view to assess execution. It also takes a press box view to understand how the components are aligned and the extent to which adjustments are necessary to improve execution. Now comes the hard part. How do you maintain alignment with today's rate of change?

Alignment Assessment

As either a team leader or team member, think of two recent team situations: one where the team performed well and met the desired outcomes; one where the team execution was below par and outcomes were not reached as intended. Use the high-performance model to analyze how the elements were aligned in the first case, and what elements were misaligned or missing in the second case. Think about how you can engage the team in these debriefs and how to create and implement recommendations arising from each situation.

Builds an Adaptive Organization

Change is hard because people overestimate the value of what they have-and underestimate the value of what they may gain by giving that up.
Belasco and Stayer

I can remember in the early 1990s when my business partners and I began to see a growing request from our clients to deal with the topic of "change management." The concept was more than a decade old by that time.[17] To a great extent it was the growth in technology that drove the need for organizations to innovate and change. The big six accounting firms at the time and management gurus such as Gary Hamel branded the concepts of change management and re-engineering to address the needs organizations had to deal with, particularly those related to technology.[18] At the time, change seemed like a wild horse that could be tamed. You could coral it, work with it, and one day ride off into the sunset. It was as if change could be captured.

Change as a Constant

If change in the nineties was algebra, today it's calculus. It is the rate of change that is making it "uncorallable," less manageable, and more difficult to isolate. John Kotter, a noted authority in the field of organizational change, echoes what is different today. He explains why the concept of *managing* change is limited and why we need to focus on *leading* change:

> I am often asked about the differences in "change management" and "change leadership," and whether it's just a matter of semantics. These terms are not interchangeable. This distinction between the two is actually quite significant. Change management, which is the term most everyone uses, refers to a set of basic tools or structures intended to keep any change effort under control. The goal is often to minimize the distractions and impacts of change. Change leadership, on the other hand, concerns the driving forces, visions, and processes that fuel large-scale transformation . . . . Change leadership is more associated with putting an engine on the whole process and making it go faster, smarter, more efficiently . . . . It's more about urgency. It's more about masses of people who want to make something happen. It's more about big visions. It's more about empowering lots and lots of people. Change leadership has the potential to get things a little bit out of control.[19]

The Kotter Approach for Leading Change Initiatives

In addition to the concept, Kotter has also developed a process for leading change. Consider this example. Your business has lost a major client because of huge mistakes including incorrect orders, missed shipments, and lack of oversight for the account. You are concerned that other major customers will also defect because of mounting problems. You have worked through these concerns with your leadership team, and as part of a retention strategy, there is a new enterprise software system that has to be implemented. Without effective leadership, this initiative has all the early warning signs of failure that disruption, frustration, and resistance signal. You invoke the words of Gene Kranz, from the film *Apollo 13*: "Failure is not an option."[20]

Your plan is to use the Kotter model to make sure you and your team can lead this change effectively. The process consists of eight steps:[21]

1. *Start with a sense of urgency*

   This step has the intensity of a "burning platform."[22] It's relatively easy to get immediate attention when you lose a warehouse to a tsunami. But can you create enduring urgency from the loss of only one client at this point? You have hard data that show that other customers are having shipment problems and how seriously it's impacting your costs and potentially sales. Change is required, and the software, admittedly just one factor, is an important part of the solution. How do you get mindshare for something that will change, even disrupt, jobs and routines inside the organization? The rationale for the change is to "improve customer retention" when the buzz around the coffee maker is a resounding "we do a pretty darn good job at customer retention, thank you very much."

   Take another related example. You're on the board of a nonprofit organization that is two years into a five-year pledge from a major donor. How do you convince the board that there are *only* 1,096 days remaining to find matching funds, and that's if you count an extra day for leap year?

   As Kotter points out, "A big reason that a true sense of urgency is rare is that it's not a natural state of affairs. He has to be created and recreated."[23] Change begins with leadership that consistently bangs the drum. In *Good by Choice*, Collins describes one mechanism leaders use to get people's attention. He calls it "productive paranoia." There's Steve Ballmer, known as "Dr. Doom," who succeeded "the grand master of productive paranoia," Bill Gates, as the head of at Microsoft.[24] Both were notorious for declaring that "things could be worse" even in the calmest of times. Effective leaders ignite change with urgency, continuously articulating *why this* and *why now*. Without the urgency, customers just walk away; major donors disappear.

2. *Build a guiding coalition*

   In order to take action, a leader needs to create a critical mass of like-minded individuals. You might think that, as the ranking member of the organization, you can demand the change. However, you need a coalition that will create the urgency and lead the process. This step is crucial.

3. *Shape the vision*

A vision is literally a picture of what the future looks like. Vision inspires and transforms. The vision of a successful customer-retention strategy is a picture of the wall in the front hallway with charts of record sales figures side by side with floor to ceiling framed letters from repeat, satisfied customers. For the nonprofit board, the vision is one of five checks arriving in the same week, each for $100,000 from individuals honoring their yearly pledges.

4. *Communicate the vision over and over again*

Like any other consultant in the leadership development business, I tell my clients it is impossible to overcommunicate a change initiative.[25] Make no assumptions about what people are thinking. Reinforcing the message requires frequent two-way communication, to open doors for questions, concerns, and ultimately buy-in and commitment.

5. *Empowering others to act on the vision*

Removing roadblocks and encouraging new and different ways to take action is the leader's job in leading change.

6. *Identify quick wins and deliver on them*

Quick wins are the actions that make the vision visible and real. The ability to isolate and take a step in the desired direction is a tangible progress. Then advertise the victory, celebrate it, and move on to the next one.

7. *Consolidate improvements and stay the course*

This is the phase beyond quick wins, where organizational structures, policies, and systems change, new people are brought in and others move on, and the need for urgency remains front and center.

8. *Institutionalizing new approaches*

Psychologists talk about change in terms of assimilation and accommodation.[26] Assimilation is the process where we take something new and integrate it into our current way of thinking. Accommodation requires a new way of thinking since the current thinking cannot "digest" the change. From an organizational perspective, incremental changes can generally be assimilated into the current structure and culture. Major changes, however, require organizations to accommodate and institutionalize new approaches, meaning adopting different expectations, behaviors, and ways of doing business.

Like most successful theories in action, the Kotter model looks simple in description yet requires focus and discipline for implementation. When all is said and done, successful change occurs when the organization is supported by the right changes in behavior, and that is not an overnight process. As Kotter describes, the challenge is overcoming complacency and maintaining a real sense of urgency.[27] Perhaps, there is something more to be learned from the lessons of "Dr. Doom" and his predecessor, "the grand master of productive paranoia."

Change as Adaptation and Leadership Style

Another important element in leading change is the *leader's* ability to adapt. In terms of behavior, adaptability is based on two components: understanding the situation or task, and understanding the people involved in the situation. In Chapter 2, we examined how these particular components evolved from the research of Blake and Mouton, and subsequently Hersey and Blanchard.[28] Hersey and Blanchard created the concept of situational leadership that takes the two elements—the task itself and the maturity level of the individual(s) involved—to prescribe one of four styles of leadership and when to use them effectively:

- Telling, when someone is new to the situation or when something needs to happen quickly.
- Selling, when the situation requires both leader direction and individual buy-in.
- Participating, when the leader and the individual share in the decision making.
- Delegating, when the individual is highly skilled and only needs guidance when there's a change in priority or direction.[29]

Building on the elements of organizational climate, Spreier et al. describe six leadership styles:[30]

1. *Directive*

   This is the traditional command and control technique that is very specific with questions of who, when, and how. This style is used effectively when there is a need for immediate compliance or working with new team members to give clear, precise, nonnegotiable direction. The directive style is less effective when the team is skilled, where they construe specific instructions as micromanagement.

2. *Visionary*

   This style is also characterized as authoritative. The style is one of clear direction and an explanation for why a particular course of action is required. The "visionary" label is appropriate because the leader describes a future state, where things are headed. This style emphasizes clarity both in terms of general direction and individual responsibilities. The "authoritative" label captures something less than immediate compliance but still conveys that the leader is in charge and knows where he and the team are headed. This style is less effective when a routine or known assignment is given to a team of experienced players.

3. *Affiliative*

   This style embodies the concept of maintaining close, personal relationships. The style attends to the needs of individuals, which makes it effective in situations of personal crisis or team turmoil. The affiliative style is less effective when an individual or team is not performing to standards, or when clear direction is needed because of a change in priorities, problems, or issues.

4. *Participative*

   This style is also characterized as democratic because it uses dialogue to get buy-in and commitment. It is a highly collaborative style intended to build consensus through shared decision making. This style works well when a leader has highly skilled players. This style is less effective when immediate compliance or clarity is required.

5. *Pacesetting*

   To call pacesetting a leadership style is a bit of a stretch because there is little to no engagement on the part of the leader with an individual or team. This is like a cross-country race, where everyone lines up at the starting line, waits for the signal, and everyone, including the leader, runs to the finish line. This style is effective when a leader supervises a team of highly skilled people working on automatic pilot. Members share a sense of high standards and quality work and need little if any supervision. They can run this cross-country course in their sleep.

All too often, the pacesetter style is used by a high achiever who is put in charge of a team or organization. If everyone is running to goal and doing his or her job, no communication is required. However, when the leader thinks that standards or expectations are not met, the negative side of the pacesetter creeps in, which is a tendency to be coercive, to take over the work, or give it to someone else. The underlying premise for pacesetting is that people don't need to be told what to do and shouldn't have to be told how to do it. That's their job and that's what they get paid for. But if performance is inconsistent or doesn't meet standards, or if priorities and direction change, then the leader needs to change styles to communicate and actively engage with the team as opposed to people "getting it" on their own. When is pacesetting less effective? Most of the time.

6. *Coaching*

The term "coaching" is often used to describe a broad range of interactions between a leader and a direct report. As a leadership style, coaching is an ongoing process focused on the employee's professional development. It speaks more to the process than any one particular event. Coaching works best when there is active engagement on the employee's part. It is a highly interactive, iterative, and ongoing dialogue. It is less effective when an individual is new to the position or needs direction to accomplish specific assignments. Some may think that you "coach" someone when he or she is new, but if using this terminology, you are probably more "directive" or "authoritative" in the beginning.

Adaptive leader behavior manifests itself in different styles, from highly directive and in charge, to collaborative and shared, to employee directed. One style of leadership does not fit all situations. Style is a tool for handling change on a routine if not daily basis to continuously align expectations, people, and outcomes.

Leadership Style Self-Assessment

Activity

Reread the description of each leadership style. Then answer these questions:

1. Which style or styles do you most often use? Consider a situation when that style was most effective. Then think of a time you used that style and it was not effective. What style might you have used instead?
2. Which style or styles do you use less frequently? In what types of situation might you use these effectively?
3. Keep in mind that your use of different styles speaks to your ability to effectively impact individual and team performance regardless of the situation. Keep a log for the next 2 weeks of the situations in which you consciously use a particular leadership style and the extent to which it was effective for the situation.

Develops Talent

The third critical competency in the alignment and execution stage is the development of talent. As a philosophy, talent development is intended to get the most out of people by tapping into, developing, and unleashing individual potential and performance on the organization. While it relates to the yearly ritual of the performance review, it is much broader. Yearly appraisals typically focus on today's necessities and not tomorrow's requirements or opportunities. Talent development goes for the long haul, where faith in the future and the development of individual capability is rewarded with ongoing organizational productivity and increased capacity.[31]

As a strategy, talent development is both high reward and high risk. The reward is increased organizational competence created through a highly trained, skilled, and invested workforce. The risk is that trained talent is in high demand. They could leave the organization. They will. The reality is that everyone leaves the organization at some point. There is an upside, however.

Several years ago, I was one of several presenters at a workshop for CPA's working in business and industry. One of the other presenters was the chief financial officer (CFO) of a large telecommunication organization I had met and worked with on two previous occasions. His topic was how he transformed the finance and accounting organization into a customer-focused organization. The transformation took five years. He described how some people were let go, some new people were hired, and how everyone participated in a massive training and development initiative. His vision was not only to improve his organization's impact on the business, but to make the business "an employer of choice." After the presentation, someone asked the question that I suspect was on the minds of several people: "What happens if you train them and they leave?" His answer was immediate, clear, and resolute: "Everyone leaves at some point. But the good news is there is now a line of people at our door wanting to come work for the organization." According to this CFO, talent development has its risks, but they are outweighed by the rewards.

Leadership Requirements for Talent Development

From a leadership perspective, developing talent has five requirements:

1. Focus on an individual's strengths with laser-like intensity
2. Lead as a coach and teacher
3. Use deliberate practice to build skills that improve performance
4. Delegate for development
5. Scan the landscape for development opportunities

Laser Focus on Individual Capabilities and Strengths

Going against the grain of common practice at the time, Marcus Buckingham opened a new discussion on the topic of talent development when he asked, "Should talent development focus on improving a person's weaknesses or building a person's strengths?"[32] Buckingham asserts that talent development should be about "developing your talents, capitalizing on your strengths and managing around your weaknesses." He defines talents as those "naturally recurring patterns of thought, feeling, and behavior." The combination of talent, knowledge, and skill creates a strength, defined as "consistent near perfect performance in an activity."

With the full weight of the Gallup organization and research conducted with more than two million people at the time of publication, the concept of strengths is mainstream thinking in today's discussion of talent development.[33]

How does this approach impact a leader's responsibilities?

- First, a leader must spend the time with an employee to identify natural talents and strengths. This requires observation, focus, and attention. The intent is to identify not only a person's individual strengths, but also how they combine to create unique personal values.[34]
- Second, a leader has to identify opportunities and methods of working with that individual that capitalize on strengths.
- Third, a leader must work with the employee to understand his weaknesses and how to minimize them. The issue of working to improve a person's weaknesses is still a source of debate. In some cases, a person's weakness is easy to work around by making slight improvements or creating support systems. For example, a person who is not good with details can partner with someone whose strength is handling the specifics.[35] In other situations, it may be necessary to stop "doing" the weakness. From my experience, the issue here is one of magnitude and impact. Sometimes, a weakness or blind spot is damaging, like an individual who continuously and publicly chastises colleagues for doing "lousy work." In this case, I would argue that there is no workaround. The behavior is detrimental and needs to stop.
- Fourth, a leader must balance an individual's strengths with the needs of the organization. This is an issue of matching assignments with talent and organizational requirements with individual strengths.

Leader as Coach and Teacher

As a college basketball fan, March Madness is like Christmas for me. Growing up in my family, I was genetically wired to play my very important part in what ESPN claims is one of the top five sports rivalries of all times: Carolina-Duke basketball.[36] When Will Blythe wrote *To Hate Like This Is to Be Happy Forever: A Thoroughly Obsessive, Intermittently Uplifting, and Occasionally Unbiased Account of the Duke-North Carolina Basketball Rivalry*, I felt as if he had a front-row seat in my living room.[37] I am proud to say that I bleed Carolina blue, which Duke Fans could argue is a reason for me to never donate blood. In addition to a great rivalry and a slew of great players from both teams, there are two legendary coaches in Mike Krzyzewski of Duke, and Dean Smith, the former coach at Carolina. Each has been a remarkable coach and a less than remarkable player. We know that the best players, like the best salespeople or the best engineers, do not necessarily make the best coaches. In making the transition from player to coach and teacher, people like Dean Smith and Coach K have connected their personal success with team success. They bring value to the organization not because they played the game but because they *teach* the game and create the conditions for successful performance.

The concept of leader as coach and teacher is used more broadly than the use of "coaching" as a leadership style. The coach and teacher role in this case refers to ongoing performance and execution—the overall approach of scoping out the work, making sure assignments are clear, and working with the team and team members to execute effectively and make improvements as needed. However, the role is also "coaching" in the professional development sense by working with people individually to increase their capabilities over time.

When it comes to "on-the-field" performance, coaches succeed or fail based on their ability to

- set standards;
- clarify expectations;
- give ongoing performance feedback;
- motivate and challenge.

Set standards.   A major responsibility of the leader as a coach is to set clear goals and objectives for both the team and each individual team member. Standards mark the level of performance required for successful execution.

Clarify expectations.   A successful coach sets clear expectations. It doesn't mean that every role is clearly scripted for every possible scenario. It does mean, however, that each person needs to make sure he or she understands expectations and ask for clarity if they don't have it.

Give ongoing feedback.   Feedback is to coaching as oxygen is to breathing. As a coach, giving feedback is most effective when it

- is objective and specific, using examples to explain what did or did not happen;
- is actionable, meaning that there is an action an individual can take to continue or eliminate the behavior;
- describes the impact of the observed behavior;
- engages the receiver;
- defines next steps that commit both coach and player to take action.

Feedback is both positive and constructive, used in situations when a team or team member meets or misses the mark. Feedback ranges from the formal and planned, as in a meeting scheduled for that purpose, to the informal and spontaneous, as in a quick follow-up to a conversation. In each case, the "rules" for the previously listed feedback should be used.

Motivate and challenge.   Setting standards, clarifying expectations, and giving feedback are reflected in the daily ritual and natural way of doing business between the leader as coach and their team. The ability to motivate and challenge takes these interactions up a notch. Coaches who truly inspire others know when and how to motivate and challenge them. It's personal, a mark of personal interest and belief from the coach to the player, the leader to a direct report. It's an emotional connection made by knowing what's important to each person, and showing how their performance helps fulfill their needs and aspirations.

Use Deliberate Practice to Improve Performance

What is the one thing that Wolfgang Mozart, Jerry Rice, and Tiger Woods have most in common that has made them successful? Is it the following:

1. Superstar designation by their rivals
2. Child prodigies
3. Unique natural talents
4. Deliberate practice

Tempted to answer one of the first three responses? Geoff Colvin, author of *Talent is Overrated*, argues that the correct answer is the fourth one, deliberate practice.[38] Colvin uses examples from such fields as chess (Bobby Fisher), sports (Jerry Rice), music (Itzhak Perlman), and business (Bill Gates) to make the point that it is deliberate practice, not simply natural talent, that creates outstanding performers. Colvin bases his argument on the research conducted by Anders Ericsson and his research team:

> The search for stable heritable characteristics that could predict or at least account for the superior performance of eminent individuals has been surprisingly unsuccessful . . . . The difference between expert performers and normal adults reflects the life-long period of deliberate effort to improve performance in a specific domain.[39]

Deliberate practice is not what you see around the house every day. What Colvin describes is a unique process that has unique impact:

- It is designed specifically to improve performance
- It can be repeated "a lot"
- Feedback on the results is continuously available
- It's highly demanding mentally (even for physical endeavors)
- It's not much fun[40]

In addition to its impact on performance, Colvin argues that what makes deliberate practice powerful is that it changes how top performers think and how they see the world. When compared to average performers, top performers

- tend to see things sooner;
- understand the significance of certain indicators, such as details that might be indicative of a trend or pattern;
- look further ahead;
- make finer distinctions;
- remember more;
- know more from seeing less.[41]

You may be thinking that the concept of deliberate practice is more applicable to coaching college all-stars or teaching performance violinists than it is to leading a business or organization. Actually, the principles directly apply to the responsibilities of a leader as coach and teacher. Colvin describes how the best organizations incorporate these principles into a culture of talent development. In these organizations, you could expect to see an environment of continuous feedback, learning from failures as well as successes, going back to the drawing board, and heading down to the practice field to try it again. Deliberate practice sharpens skill sets, builds organizational capacity, and potentially impacts the ability of people to broaden their thinking horizons, to see farther down the road, to anticipate situations, and to make better decisions.[42]

Delegate for Development

Delegation is the leader's Swiss army knife. It is a unique multipurpose capability for leading change, developing talent, and creating greater organizational capacity. Delegation is generally defined as giving someone the authority to complete a task or assignment. The purpose covers a range of situations, from needing an extra pair of hands to complete a single task to the major responsibilities attached to managing a piece of the business.

Delegation is the leader's Swiss army knife. It is a unique multipurpose capability for leading change, developing talent, and creating greater organizational capacity.

In the middle of this spectrum are often opportunities for a leader to delegate assignments such as learning and development assignments.

- For example, an individual approaches a manager for how to handle a specific issue or problem. Rather than giving an answer, the manager turns the question around by asking the individual to clearly define the issue, provide supporting data, suggest options for taking action, and make a recommendation. These are the "teachable moments" that give someone experience now, making it possible to delegate these decisions or assignment to them in the future.
- There's also the "see one, do one, teach one" method of delegation, the so-called intern model used in the medical field.
- There are situations where a manager delegates responsibilities to a specific employee as part of a strategic process to broaden that individual's experience and skill set.

Effective delegation has several important benefits:

- It expands an employee's skill sets and broadens his or her capabilities.
- It motivates those who crave for new and challenging assignments.
- It enables the leader to take on more responsibility from their manager.
- It prepares successors for the roles they will one day inherit.
- It builds and expands organizational capability and competence.

Scan the Landscape for Development Opportunities

In addition to coaching, the leader is continuously on reconnaissance to find development opportunities for his or her employees for both current and future roles. While some organizations have designed on-the-job development programs, such as rotational assignments or internships, the vast majority of these are opportunistic in nature. Leaders seize on these opportunities when they have:

1. a clear understanding for what skills and experiences an individual wants and needs based on strengths, interests, and motivation;
2. a vast network and connections throughout the business;
3. good negotiation skills to secure these positions once they are located;
4. the ability to go nonlinear in terms of finding opportunities in different parts of the business that could broaden someone's strengths and talents.

The key is that the leader as coach is constantly vigilant, always on the prowl for development opportunities while motivating and challenging team members to expand their capabilities in their current roles.

Where and How Are You Spending Time as a Teacher and Coach?

Activity

In your role as the teacher and coach, you have an opportunity to favorably impact a person's career development *and* increase the capability of the team and consequently the business. Here is some food for thought for making the coaching role a priority.

1. Coaching is an interactive process for development planning and implementation with each team member with routinely scheduled coaching meetings for feedback, engagement, and measuring progress against goals.

   a) For new team members, these meetings are often directed to learning the fundamentals of the job and role, ongoing feedback, and lessons learned.
   b) For experienced individuals, coaching often takes the form of development assignments and stretch goals to provide challenging, engaging, and exciting opportunities that broaden an individual's base of expertise and credibility.

c) For the seasoned professional, it's focusing on where that individual is headed, broadening that person's visibility across the business, and developing the skills and experiences needed to have a broader impact on the business.

2. Effective coaching is a function of both the amount and quality of time spent in professional development for the purposes of increased personal competence.

Do the math: To what extent are you spending time teaching and coaching each individual team member on a routine basis? Weekly? Monthly? Quarterly? Yearly? None of the above? Do not count weekly project updates or problem resolution meetings *unless* a portion of that time is devoted to feedback, skill development, and lessons learned.

Recommendation: Spending one hour monthly with each person or the equivalent of three hours quarterly coaching each individual is a manageable and solid routine.

3. Is there a development plan with professional development goals for each team member? These are not the functional or business goals needed in the annual performance appraisal. These are specifically dedicated to skill, competency, and behavioral development to improve and expand personal capability. Harness the impact of goals because they create action, intent, and specificity.

4. A good development plan consists of

- two to three *SMART* goals;

  If you are not familiar with *SMART*, an effective goal must be specific, measurable, actionable, relevant, and time-phased. An often used example is the statement that "I want to lose weight," a desirable state but not a *SMART* goal. "I am going to lose 10 pounds in the next 60 days by watching my diet and working out at the YMCA five times per week"—now that's *SMART*, in more ways than one.

- a statement of the desired impact;
- specific development activities for specific and deliberate practice;
- measures of success.

Table 4.1 Professional development goal example

SMART development goal	Desired impact	Development activities	Measure of success
To increase my presentation capability by presenting to three different audiences on the need for changes in the tech transfer process by December 15.	Address each audience at his or her level of understanding and with specific implications for his or her area	- Attend the Effective Presentation training course that includes video-taped feedback on June 30 - Observe at least one presentation at a meeting conducted by an outstanding presenter in our organization, such as Dr. Koonce - Create a draft presentation - Review the outline with my manager for structure, content, and how to frame for each audience - Prep for each presentation by meeting with at least one member from each audience in advance to get his or her input - Practice using clear, concise, and relevant language and examples	Follow-up with at least one member from each group for their feedback and recommendations

Table 4.1 is an example of a professional development goal using SMART criteria.

5. While your role as coach is critical, the accountability for the professional development plan rests with the team member. You and the organization provide the context and opportunity for development. When the team member takes ownership of his or her development, it's a win–win outcome all the way around.

Leads by Example

"The Shocker: I Am the Problem"

Successful leaders know that others scrutinize their behavior, sometimes their every move. They know this comes with the territory and use this knowledge to their advantage. They understand their impact on others and use their *presence* to lead by example.[43]

To lead by example is to lead with intent. Ralph Stayer, the chief executive officer (CEO) of Johnsonville Sausage, is one person who understands what this means.[44] Stayer describes how he came to the realization that the "victim mentality" he had demonstrated over the years was mirrored throughout his organization. One day it hit him. Stayer realized that he had to make the change "from being a victim to being responsible." The question he asked himself: "What am I doing or not doing that causes the situation I don't like?" As a result, Stayer changed his behavior to demonstrate what he expected others to do, to take responsibility and ownership over what they could control, or to influence the situation for a favorable outcome when they didn't. "No more 'victimitis.'" Stayer modeled the behavior he expected of others. Today these behaviors are imbedded in the culture known as the Johnsonville Way. And it started with one shocking realization: "I am the problem."[45]

Chapter Summary

Mentoré leadership stage comparisons

Expertise stage	Credibility stage	Alignment & execution stage
What	Who	How
Track record	Image & reputation	Coaching & leading by example
Knowledge & experience	Communication & influence	Decision making, prioritization & problem resolution
Depth	Breadth	Agility
Student of knowledge	Student of people	Student of the organization
Native intelligence	Emotional intelligence	Systems thinking
How smart you are	How you deliver value to others in the organization	How to maximize operational efficiencies
Knowing your subject matter	Knowing your audience	Knowing your organization

Taking Stock

- Moving into the stage of alignment and execution is a Rubicon moment in leadership development. It's not simply moving beyond building expertise and credibility into what's next, nor is it only about just executing differently. The move requires a different way of thinking with different competencies for a different purpose—to build the capability and capacity of the organization and to manage your piece of the business.

- Having to work through others in the contemporary world is no longer just because you have a team or organization reporting to you. Managing projects, leading cross-functional initiatives, and simply the day-to-day maneuvering in a matrix environment require working through people who *don't* report to you.

- One of the biggest misconceptions high achievers have when they manage a team is that they have to be super achievers, who need to know more, do more, or oversee every detail of the work like they would do if they were doing it alone. The problem is that they're not doing it alone, and the tendency to micromanage heads them down a slippery slope.

- Success in the alignment and execution stage is simultaneously stepping up, taking on more responsibility for your piece of the business, and letting go, no longer having to be the best student in the class.

- Working in this stage asks the question how—how do we achieve results?

- It's always about execution, looking at on-the-field performance. The important perspective in alignment and execution, however, is also from "the press box," to see how the elements of the team or organization align and determine if adjustments are needed.

- The landscape of an organization is defined by (a) its culture, how people relate; (b) its operations, how business processes relate; and (c) how the culture and operations interrelate.

- Culture defines a way of doing business, how people are treated, what's valued and important, and what gets recognized, rewarded, and reinforced. The culture is created, reinforced, or changed through behavior that reflect the desired values, not simply by espousing the values.

- The *Good to Great* companies researched by Collins give us a clear understanding that cultures are definable entities that produce measurable outcomes. Leadership effectiveness can also have an impact on the type of culture that's created.[46]
- Organizational climate is a measure of how people experience the organization. Organizations measure climate through the dimensions of flexibility, responsibility, standards, clarity, rewards, and team commitment. Clarity is the one characteristic most closely associated with personal and organizational productivity.
- Analytical thinking and emotional intelligence are critical thought processes in the stages of building a leadership base, but in this stage, systems thinking is also required.
- The high-performance organization is a systems model for analyzing organizational effectiveness and understanding the impact of change. The system is composed on the elements of leadership, organization, jobs, and people. The leader's role is to monitor both the external business environment and the organization, to realign the elements as required, and to understand how adjustments impact overall execution.
- Managing change and leading change are not differences in semantics; they represent two different approaches. Managing change looks to control change as it enters the system. Leading change looks to turbo charge change through the system. John Kotter's model for leading change is a pragmatic approach that starts with a sense of urgency and a coalition of supporters to create quick victories. These are augmented with ongoing communication and the consolidation of small wins into the "new" way of doing business.
- Leaders adapt by making adjustments in their styles for how they lead. They understand that the situation and people involved determine what style of leadership—from providing specific direction to allowing the team to call the shots—is best.

- The leader as coach and teacher moves an organization from managing performance to developing talent. Good leaders are good coaches who know how to "teach the game" and motivate individuals to achieve. Their interest is personal and it shows. They know that good talent is highly marketable and at one point good talent moves on. They also believe that as talent developers they can attract the best players. Talent leaves, and new talent walks in the door.

- Deliberate practice is a methodical process for developing skills and acquiring competencies in an environment of continuous learning, application, and feedback. Over time, deliberate practice can change how someone thinks, to see more from less, to anticipate, and to make better decisions.

- Delegation is the multipurpose leadership tool that broadens individual capabilities, prepares successors, and expands organizational capacity.

- In addition to delegating assignments for development, a leader needs to be ever vigilant for team member development opportunities both inside and outside the functional organization.

- As a leader, people take their cues not from what you say but from what you do. If the two don't line up, they go with what you do. Leading by example is acting in the manner that you expect of others. It speaks to your presence, stature, and image.

CHAPTER 5

Stage Four: Strategy

Bolting Down to Infinity

Life in the Third Dimension

Comedians Mel Brooks and Carl Reiner created a comic routine in 1961 called the "2000 year old man." In one skit, Reiner asks Mel Brooks, born in the BC era and living today, if he always prayed to the Almighty. Brooks said that was not always the case. In the early days, they used to pray to a guy named Phil. Then one day the sky opened up and a lightning bolt struck and killed Phil. At that point, Brooks recalls, we knew that "there's somebody bigger than Phil."[1]

Every organization has its own Phil moment. Consider the economic events in 2008: some businesses did not survive. Such situations demonstrate how forces outside the organization's control have a catastrophic effect on what happens inside the system. Organizations must look beyond their boundaries and scan the external horizon. It means going beyond how the system works to the external factors and why these factors are uniquely important. Moving from how to why is a big step. In the alignment and execution stage, a leader *looks down* into the organizational system; in the strategy stage, a leader looks *up and outside* the system and asks why—why are we doing what we do?

Think about the evolution of leadership to this point. In the expertise stage, a leader learns to poke and prod on the current reality—to see it, understand it, and digest it. Analytical thinking and curiosity work together to build a base of knowledge and experience. This keeps you grounded. Life in the expertise stage is predictable, bolted down.

The transition into the credibility stage requires emotional intelligence—to study people and understand what makes them tick. You focus

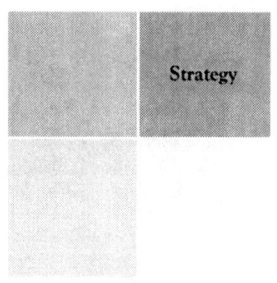

Strategy stage

Strategy is engaging in strategic leadership which requires looking out beyond organizational or functional boundaries to understand the bigger picture and the business.

Mentoré strategy competencies

Strategic thinker: the ability to see the big picture by thinking broadly and extrapolating from current to future trends and outcomes

Walks in the customer's shoes: creates and develops a customer dialogue that can involve all levels of the organization

Business partner and strategist: works as partner and positions the organization to deliver value through ongoing commitment and shared risk for the success of the end-customer; strives for win–win–win outcomes

Business savvy: a potent mix of strategic thinking and business acumen with experience and insight that yields a confidence for moving smartly to the future

on building trust, increasing visibility, communicating and influencing others effectively, and delivering something of value so that others succeed. As expertise and credibility build on each other, they create a track record of success and increase personal capability and competence. The combination of native intelligence and emotional intelligence makes you smarter. The organization needs this type of smartness.

Then there's a leap into alignment and execution where the organization asks you to run a part of the business. Your value needs to be exponential—to increase organizational capacity by accomplishing work through others. This requires a change in focus, to look at the dynamics of change rather than strictly an analytical, cause-effect perspective. You head up to the press box to get a better view of how all the moving parts work together, and how alignment impacts overall performance. You tinker, adjust, reassess, and execute. Change, once a stranger, is now your next-door neighbor. Nothing is bolted down; by design, people, processes, and structure are held together by Velcro. It's a mix-and-match world.

But there is more. Change is a constant force in the organization. While we are told that the world out there is smaller, the world in here, inside the business, seems bigger. The only way that leadership can accommodate the impact of change is to expand in yet a third dimension—understanding the business in the context of the bigger picture. This is not a conceptual argument. It is motivated by a need to see a future direction and path forward. It's also motivated by fear—that success in the present may not translate to success or even existence in the future. Heads-down leadership affirms, "How do we get better today?" Head's up leadership asks, "Will we be around tomorrow?" What has happened to the use of instamatic cameras for everyday pictures? Gone. Onion skin and carbon paper? Gone. ZAP mail? Gone. Typewriters, rotary phones, Univac computers, dinosaurs, eight track tapes, Spin and Marty, Vaudeville? All gone. It is easy to say *change or die.* But that does not help understand why change is needed and how organizations and businesses evolve to make it to tomorrow.

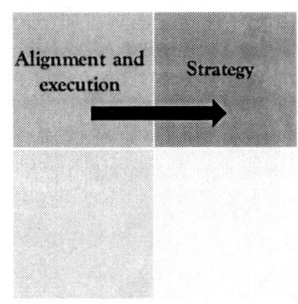

What Is Different?

Leadership at this strategic level is unique. The strategic competencies have more to do with how you think and view the world than simply the behaviors you adopt. Leadership in this stage requires

1. a *broader* perspective, strategic thinking, and the ability to see the bigger picture;
2. a *different* perspective, the ability to walk in your customer's shoes;

3. a *new* perspective, to work as a partner and strategist to the business;

4. an *integrated* perspective, whole-brain thinking that leads to being business savvy.

Strategic Thinking: A Broader Perspective

What Is Strategic Thinking?

A leader must commit to that which has not yet happened.

Roger Nierenberg

To begin with, an explanation of what something is *not* is to acknowledge the confusion for what something is. This is the approach Professor Jeanne M. Liedtka describes in "Strategic Thinking: Can It Be Taught?"[2] Liedtka contends that strategic thinking is often viewed as thinking about strategy. Strategic thinking, however, is not strategy or strategic planning. Strategy, as we will explore, is a proposed course of action that gives direction and a sorting mechanism for what an organization will, and conversely, will not do. Several management experts including Mintzberg (1994),[3] Nasi (1991),[4] and Hamel and Prahalad (1994)[5] clearly articulate the difference between strategic thinking and strategic planning. Mintzberg, for one, argued that strategic planning is an "analytical process for programming already identifiable strategies." Strategic thinking, however, is "a synthesis process, utilizing intuition and creativity" whose outcome is "an integrated perspective of the enterprise."[6]

Liedtka, like Mintzberg, describes strategic thinking as a thinking process, not the business process of strategic planning.[7] Liedtka identifies five distinct qualities:

1. *A systems perspective*

This is the same type of thinking described in the alignment and execution stage. Liedtka adds, however, that there is the need to look outside the boundaries of the system at those factors that impact what is inside. Much like a bigger picture, there is a bigger system that encompasses the system in question.

2. *Intent-focused*

   According to Hamel and Prahalad,[8] strategic intent conveys

   a) a sense of direction—a competitively unique position;

   b) a sense of discovery—a promise of exploration;

   c) a sense of destiny—an emotional commitment.

3. *Intelligent opportunism*

   While intent drives direction, there is also a need to look at alternatives and to keep options open as part of the conversation.

4. *Thinking in time*

   Thinking in time is a way to connect the present and the future.

5. *Hypothesis-driven*

   Liedtka argues that strategic thinking is an iterative process best served by hypothesis testing and the scientific method of discovery.

Strategic Thinking and Chaos Theory

As Dr. T. Irene Sanders tells the story, on a winter day in 1961, Dr. Edward Lorenz, a Massachusetts Institute of Technology research meteorologist and mathematician, walked away from his desk to grab a cup of coffee.[9] He had just plugged numbers into a weather forecasting model on his computer as he normally did, or so he thought. When he returned, what he saw would change the way scientists think about the future. Instead of the normal pattern, Lorenz saw something different, wilder fluctuations than ever before. Had he done anything differently? In thinking back over his routine, he realized he made one small change, which was rounding off 1 of 12 variables, from 0.506127 to 0.506. To paraphrase Neil Armstrong's 1969 famous moon-landing quote, "that's one small rounding step for a scientist, one giant leap for science."[10]

Lorenz is considered the father of chaos theory, which sounds totally devoid of scientific reasoning but is actually quite the opposite. What Lorenz discovered was that the forecast for the weather in Boston tomorrow, for example, is not based solely on the weather in Milwaukee today. That's because it does not take into account a multitude of factors that could change the weather pattern. Lorenz postulated that these changes are nonlinear, but because these changes are rooted in the present, they are less than random and subject to some level of predictability. He refers to the present conditions as initiating conditions. The pattern that results from the initiating conditions and their transformation caused by the other change-related factors is called the butterfly effect, named in part from a paper Lorenz wrote and from the basic shape of the pattern itself.[11] Lorenz argues that the future (tomorrow's weather in Boston) is based on known initiating conditions (today's weather in Milwaukee) and their sensitivity to certain forces in their path (the jet stream and a weather front moving up the East Coast).[12]

Principles of Strategic Thinking

It may be described as chaos, but the concept of thinking about the future based on the current reality is critical to what it means to think strategically. Using the Lorenz legacy and her own research, Dr. Sanders describes four key strategic thinking principles:

1. The future is rooted in the present. Seeing the future in today's reality is the power of *insight*. Insights are often spontaneous flashes that seem to appear from nowhere.
2. Looking to the future requires an understanding of "the creative potential and sensitivity to new influences." Sanders refers to these influences as perking conditions.
3. Strategic thinking is an interplay of the right brain with the left brain, the combination of the creative with the analytical.
4. Strategic thinking is visual thinking. It is the ability literally to see the future based on a pattern of thought. As Sanders explains, "The biggest difference between those who receive spontaneous insights and those who are known to be visual thinkers is that visual thinkers consciously nurture the process of insight. They use their imaginations to engage both intuition and intellect."[13] However, the fact that you *see* it does not mean that others see and understand it. Herein lies one of the biggest challenges in strategic leadership: the ability to translate visual thinking into a vision and picture that others see and comprehend.[14]

Like Lorenz, Sanders helps us understand the need to think of the future as an extrapolation of the current reality. Making this connection is thinking strategically, "the skill that will allow us to see and influence the future, today."[15] While the future may appear random and unpredictable, there is "a type of self-organizing pattern, shape, or structure that becomes obvious when the behavior of the system is seen as a whole. There is order hidden beneath the disorder."[16]

"Thinking Without Thinking"

Insight, Foresight, and Intuition

How is it that a former tennis pro turned coach, Vic Braden, can predict when a player will double fault with uncanny accuracy? How can an orthopedic surgeon in Boston look at a magnetic resonance image (MRI) of my shoulder and instantaneously say "your shoulder is trashed," or my border collie Millie know exactly where I was going to kick a ball the minute it left my foot? Ask Malcom Gladwell.[17] It seems that some people (and dogs) have the ability to see more from less, a process for turning flashes of insight into successful predictions for the future. Similar to what happens through deliberate practice and visual thinking, some people use their experience and insight to tell them what to expect. At one time it may have been a conscious thought process built on long hours of observation and study. But over time it becomes unconscious, where the whole picture is captured in the smallest detail. As Gladwell explains, for these people it may begin as a flash, first impression, or snap judgment, but in time the ability to zero in on the unexplainable is continuously decoded. Gladwell adds, "Whenever we have something we are good at— something we care about—that experience and passion fundamentally change the nature of our first impressions." What we are building is a "data-base of the unconscious."[18]

Collectively, Liedtka, Sanders, and Gladwell describe a way of thinking we have not encountered to this point in the evolution of leadership. What's different, important, and unique about this process are the following characteristics. Strategic thinking

- is nonlinear but has some degree of predictability;
- starts in the present and links to the future;
- has the capacity to shape a forward direction;

- is thinking with the whole brain, a combination of logic and emotion;
- has the capability to see more from less;
- envelops risk taking and innovation as part of the process rather than separate disciplines;
- is continuously reinforced through a unique blend of experience and insight that moves from conscious to unconscious thought;
- embraces insight, foresight, and intuition as leadership principles, not psychological concepts.

How to Think Strategically

A good hockey player plays where the puck is. A great hockey player plays where the puck is going to be.
Wayne Gretzky

Strategic thinking begins with the ability to step back from the day-to-day routine, to better understand what is going on, and to ask why things are happening as they do. The capacity to think strategically is strengthened by focusing on three major components:

1. *Anticipation*

   To anticipate is to realize something before it happens, to be proactive. Anticipation shapes the front end of strategic thinking because it puts your mind on alert for what to expect, to factor in next steps (the future) based on an understanding of past situations and current experience. Anticipation and proactive thinking are good mental calisthenics for thinking outside the current reality.

2. *Extrapolation*

   In mathematical terms, extrapolation is "an estimation of a value based on extending a known sequence of values or facts beyond the area that is certainly known."[19] From a strategic thinking perspective, extrapolation is the process of projecting out from the present situation to a future point *beyond* known next steps. As a strategic thinking capability, there are two types of extrapolation: (a) by plotting a linear-type trajectory from here to there or (b) by plotting a nonlinear course defined by using a reference point in a different dimension, in this case, the future. A linear-type trajectory is the extrapolation *from the current to the future* based on movement along the same path. Moving from desktop computers to laptops illustrates such movement. The introduction of a reference point in the future, however, creates a different dynamic. Instead of plotting the future based on a linear trajectory, the *future reference point* defines a different, unique, and nonlinear path for moving forward. Think of the introduction of the iPhone in 2007, a combination of an iPod, computer, phone, and camera wrapped into one product. The reference point in this case is the vision of such a device that fits in and is operated by your hand. The combination of four devices into a hand-held and operated device created a different, unique, and nonlinear path forward from the current state of technology at that time.[20]

Asking "What If?"

Nonlinear extrapolation may sound more complicated than intended. It uses a similar line of inquiry introduced in curiosity, one of the fundamental competencies in the expertise stage. This is asking the question, what if. Admittedly, curiosity in the context of the big picture is operating in rarified air, where seeing something that is not visible today is held in the palm of millions of hands tomorrow. The what if question opens the door to taking risks, thinking creatively, and looking beyond the constraints imposed by the current reality. Asking what if shakes any degree of certainty created by moving from the known present to the predictable future. Perhaps, this type of thinking is the reason why Lorenz was tagged with discovering a theory of chaos.

Vision

Extrapolation is expressed through vision. Vision is a picture of what success looks like in the future. A picture is not simply words and concepts. I can describe the process of the sun rising over the Grand Canyon to you, or I can show you a picture. Which is more impactful? The power of vision is that you see it, you help others see it, and they help others to see it as well.

As a leader, a vision must connect emotionally with those around you. A good place to start is the development of a simple statement of a vision for your part of the business. Consider the following:

- How do you define the role of your group?
- What is the value that your group creates for the business?
- What is the guiding principle that you can point to that gives meaning to any activity in which you or your group are engaged, that answers the question why—why are we doing this activity?
- What does success look like?
- As a result of that success, what would you see? This is the picture that you're looking to create.

3. *Translation*

Translation is the process that converts strategic thinking into concrete action. Without action, strategic thinking can easily be construed as nothing more than fortune telling. The process of translation is similar to Liedtka's description of hypothesis testing, a unique blend of analytical thinking and creative problem solving.[21] But what's strikingly different about translation is the ability to describe the present in the future tense, and the future in the present tense. If this sounds a lot like strategy, it's because it is.

Strategy: Applying Strategic Thinking to the Business

Change or die? How about "be strategic or be gone." Richard Horwath, author and expert in the field of strategy and strategic thinking, describes an urgency that is echoed throughout the business world. Horwath defines strategic thinking as "the generation and application of business insights on a continual basis to achieve global competitive advantage."[22] Thinking strategically, according to Horwath, requires the three As: acumen through insight, allocation of resources, and action. Insight relates to business outcomes.[23] Strategic insight requires a deeper dive, which means to search for deeper insight by connecting known information in different ways. Horwath's sources of insight are understanding the context of the business, talking to customers, and using conceptual models to transform information into understanding.[24]

Like Sanders, Horwath creates a line of sight from the present to the future. Uniquely, however, is how Horwath links strategic thinking to business:

- First there is insight.
- Insight leads to foresight.
- Foresight creates differentiation and defines direction.
- Direction creates choices.
- Choices define allocation of limited resources.

In short, Horwath defines strategy as "the intelligent allocation of limited resources through a unique system of activities to outperform the competition in serving customers."[25]

Jack Welch, former chief executive officer (CEO) of General Electric, equates strategy with a straightforward, unambiguous plan for winning:

- "Strategy means making clear-cut choices about how to compete. You cannot be everything to everybody, no matter what the size of your business and how deep its pockets."
- "In real life, strategy is actually very straightforward. You pick a general direction and implement like hell."
- "If you're headed in the right direction and are broad enough, strategies don't really need to change all that often."[26]

It would be remise to discuss strategy without considering Michael Porter. Porter's principles, which are widely studied and responsible for much of the current thinking on the topic, reflect several of the themes previously mentioned:

- Strategy is not operational effectiveness.
- Strategy is about being different. "It means deliberately choosing a different set of activities to deliver a unique mix of value."[27]

- A sustainable strategic position requires trade-offs. Deliberate choices have to be made.
- The concept of fit represents an operational chain where everything counts. Fit drives both competitive advantage and sustainability. There are no weak or unnecessary links.
- Organizations need to rediscover strategy. Looking at operational effectiveness is seductive because of the push for measurable results. Yet, without strategy to guide choice, organizations engage in activities that may or may not align to the future direction.[28]

Walking in Your Customer's Shoes: A Different Perspective

As Horwath points out, customers are one of the most important forces that shape the business landscape. They are an important source of insight. A customer is an individual or group to whom you and your organization provide products and services. From an enterprise perspective, customers break out into two groups: internal, meaning inside your organization and downstream from where you sit, and external, the ultimate consumers of what your organization delivers, the people who write the checks that enable you to pay your bills. Walking in your customer's shoes is different from customer focus. "Walking in their shoes" begins with *your customer.* It is a way for you to connect emotionally with them by looking out at the world through *their* eyes, to understand and experience the world as they do. Customer focus, on the other hand, implies that the perspective begins with *you.* Focusing on the customer is a good start, but, without the drive to dig deeper for customer understanding, the nature of the relationship tends to be only transactional.

The ability to walk in your customer's shoes is important for three reasons. First, it is a big credibility builder. Building credibility takes time, but the time represents a *deliberate investment.* Credibility opens communication, and communication leads to understanding and insight. Second, it gives you a perspective of how your customer sees the world, a perspective that also includes how they see you. Third, it enables you and your organization to anticipate future needs, look for future opportunities, and translate customer data into strategy and action steps.

The Power of Dialogue

The ability to understand your customers, both internal and external, happens best through dialogue. Dialogue is a process of engagement intended to build relationships through mutual understanding. Daniel Yankelovich, noted public opinion expert and social scientist, describes dialogue as a process needed to bridge the understanding gap and facilitate a level of engagement "that is missing in contemporary American society."[29] Yankelovich credits theoretical physicist David Bohm as one of dialogue's original thinkers: "To his own surprise, Bohm learned that world-class physicists develop their most creative ideas not in solitary thought but through dialogue with one another."[30] Peter Senge, an expert in organizational development and learning, states that dialogue is essential to team learning, "the capacity of members of a team to suspend assumptions and enter into a genuine thinking together."[31] In addition, the unique capability created through the process of dialogue is ideally suited to engage both internal and external customers.

Dialogue Fundamentals

Engaging in customer dialogue is not confined to a particular form or format, but there are several guidelines to consider:

1. *Preparation*
   Preparation speaks to intent: What are you looking to understand and accomplish through these discussions? Preparation includes thinking about purpose and outcomes, who needs to be a part of this process, what topics to pursue, and what questions to ask.
2. *The proper framing*
   Setting expectations for the process with your customers is critical. While the immediate need is often to solve problems or resolve issues, the long-term objective is to create a structure for open communication and commitment to mutually beneficial outcomes.

Framing should also include important ground rules for open communication and feedback: the use of objective observations and specific examples, the discussion of impact, and engagement in problem solving, not personal attacks or blame.

3. *Use of probing, open-ended questions*

This may seem like a small detail, but these questions are extremely important to the process. Questions such as "What is the biggest challenge you face in the coming year?" "How do you and your organization measure success?" or "What are your customer's biggest challenges?" are the types of questions that open up a deeper discussion of what is critical and important. Obviously, the specific questions will depend on the overall purpose, and it is important to create these questions ahead of time.

4. *Active listening*

Active listening is the skill that never goes away. This skill never goes away. In any conversation with customers, and particularly these conversations, the key is listening. Listening builds trust. This does not mean you have to agree with your customer's point of view. It does mean you have to understand it.

5. *Taking action*

At some point, the dialogue process yields a set of actions that can range from resolving problems, taking corrective actions, generating new ideas, to taking unprecedented next steps. A successful process reinforces desired outcomes, and successful outcomes reinforce the value of the process.

Dialogue as Discovery and Action

Dialogue is a process of discovery where you can anticipate three types of opportunities that call for action, sometimes immediate, sometimes over a period of time. These take the form of

1. problem resolution;
2. feedback;
3. heart-to-heart discussions.

1. Resolving problems and issues is perhaps the most common and most transactional level of customer interaction. Problem resolution is a reactive and essential process. It is typically measured by (a) the timeliness and level of the response, and (b) the effectiveness of the solution. Timeliness and responsiveness are critical behaviors that, over time, build credibility in the customer's eyes. Where ongoing dialogue helps turn the corner on problem resolution is through problem *anticipation*. This is clearly more proactive, intended to mitigate problems in advance. It also pushes deeper into issues by looking at root causes and patterns, which, if understood, can eradicate problems before they develop. As the clean version of the bumper sticker says, problems happen, so having an effective and timely resolution process is essential. Anticipation, on the other hand, is a more strategic and potentially longer-term solution.

2. The second opportunity for dialogue is to ask for and give feedback. This could be feedback regarding a specific situation or initiative, or it could be more generalized over a period of time. Both are opportunities for proactive, in-depth discussions. One example is the project postmortem. Properly framed, this discussion enables you and your customer to put all issues on the table, such as successes and frustrations, lessons learned, and what to do differently next time. These discussions are a mix of facts and perceptions, objective data, and personal needs. Like any other type of dialogue, the goal is understanding, not agreement. The purpose is to pinpoint what is critical for all parties and to strategize about how to move forward together in the future.

3. The heart-to-heart discussion is the most intimate and at the deepest level of the dialogue process. Getting to the level of what is fundamentally important for you, your customers, and your business partners—both now and moving forward—can grow out of an open and ongoing process for problem solving and feedback. This is not to say, however, that you shouldn't set aside a particular time to have a heart-to-heart discussion. These discussions are particularly important under two conditions: when there is an obvious mismatch of expectations, and when there is a specific need to take the

relationship to a higher level. Whether it's an ongoing process or a particular discussion, the purpose is the same, that is, to go to a deeper level of what's truly important.

The pattern for customer dialogue that have been observed most often is the evolution described earlier. It begins with working through thorny problems first. In time, problem resolution and problem anticipation evolve into discussions for improving processes. Both sides ask for and get feedback on a regular basis. Somewhere in this mix, the needs for proactive communication, sharing critical information, setting expectations, and clarifying roles and responsibilities emerge. If all parties stay the course, they build a successful track record together. The combination of achieving success, learning from failure, and maintaining an open dialogue create an invaluable framework for understanding and commitment.

Dialogue as Horizontal Alignment and Beyond

With some variation, the process of dialogue applies to both internal and external customers. What's similar is that the basic purpose, components, and levels of discovery of the process applies equally to both groups. What's different, however, is what organizational elements the dialogue impacts and the benefits that are accrued.

Crossing Borders

Utilizing the process of dialogue with internal customers means crossing functional borders. Functional organizations, by design, are vertically integrated and subject to their unique gravitational pull. On the one hand, vertical integration creates focus. On the other hand, that focus is directed down and inside the organization. While functional borders define scope and clarify responsibilities, they also create jurisdictions where one function ends and another begins. Different jurisdictions have different priorities, responsibilities, and commitments. The greater the internal focus, the tougher it is to move across borders.

Additionally, what makes the dialogue process particularly difficult inside the same business organization are the expectations people have for each other and the politics that comes with different jurisdictions. On the one hand, many people *expect* that since everyone works for the same business, they *should* share the same level of responsibility, priority, and commitment. When people do not see that, they are less tolerant and more agitated than they might be with someone from the outside. Then there's that nagging perception that jurisdictional politics is a zero-sum game, one with known winners and losers. These perceptions start changing when strategic functional leaders willfully engage in dialogue with other functional leaders to overcome differences and resolve territorial disputes. What the dialogue process impacts is horizontal *alignment*, and the potential outcome is a more unified understanding of the business. As the number of successful border crossings increase, the opportunities to streamline processes and communication increase, and the potential to improve bottom-line performance increases as well.

Defining the Third Win

When compared with internal customers, dialogue with external customers varies in three ways.

First, as mentioned earlier, there seems to be more tolerance when engaged with external customers. No doubt this is driven in part by the higher risk of engaging directly with those who use your products and services and write checks to your business and ultimately to you. Nonetheless, the proactive nature of dialogue with external customers, whether directed at problem resolution, problem anticipation, mutual feedback, or the discovery of critical long-term needs, creates a context of openness, mutual respect, and win–win outcomes. Second, successful dialogue with external customers can increase new business opportunities and improve efficiencies across both organizations. This impacts both top and bottom-line performance.

Third, when engaged with external customers, there is a potential line of sight from you, to your customers, and to *their customers*. The benefit here is the opportunity to see beyond win–win outcomes by defining the win for the *customer's customer*: the win–win–*win*. When you and your customer are focused on the third win, there is a point of mutual alignment and far-reaching benefit. When you experience what your customer experiences, you are in a better position to apply that knowledge to provide better products, better services, and better solutions. On the relationship-building side, you're in it together.

It is not as easy to see the third win when looking internally, meaning inside the business. When that line of sight exists, however, it has all the power that strategy has to offer. It impacts and is impacted by horizontal alignment that extends across the organization, to the boundary of the business and across directly to customers. Differences arise when the line of sight is less visible for some groups deep inside the organization, particularly where their priorities and metrics have no apparent connection with customer outcomes. This is why crossing internal borders is critical. Ultimately, dialogue and alignment reinforce each other, and their combined power is critical for strategic success.

Working As a Partner and Strategist to the Business: A New Perspective

From Cooperation to Collaboration to Partnering

While the concepts for cooperation, collaboration, and partnering are often used interchangeably, they represent different levels of engagement and ownership for results.

Cooperation is generally defined as working together to the same end. Cooperation emphasizes how people work together to reach a common objective. It's possible that people can work together cooperatively but have different levels of commitment to the outcome. Collaboration, like cooperation, seeks good working relationships. What's different with collaboration, however, is a greater emphasis on outcomes and creation of mutual benefit. We think of collaboration as a win–win situation. Each person or organization in the relationship may not measure success in the same way, but each commits to the outcome and understands that *both* must benefit for the relationship to succeed. In collaboration, commitment and engagement work in parallel.

Partnering represents yet a different and unique level of engagement. Using the concept of the third win, partners strive for outcomes that are beneficial to each other *and* to the customer whom they have in common: I win, my partner wins, and the customer wins. Partners make it a point to learn about each other's business and the impact that each has on the other. Partnering looks and behaves differently from other relationships because each partner makes a deeper, longer-term commitment to meet each other's needs and the needs of their customer, both now and in the future. It means sharing the risks as well as the rewards. Working as a partner, therefore, also requires a strategic perspective; the focus is less on partner-specific measures of success and more on shared measures of customer success.

Achieving Status As Partner and Strategist

One of the more common references to achieving a desired level of organizational status is "getting a seat at the table." Thinking about status takes us back to the role of credibility in leadership development. Status is like credibility in two ways: (1) it is based on the perception of others, and (2) it is not so much an end state as it is an indication of a particular level of perceived value.

Attaining the status of partner and strategist doesn't start in the strategy stage of leadership development. It actually begins as part of the track record of success you create through personal competence, a combination of expertise and credibility. You build your leadership resumé through increased organizational impact on alignment and execution, meaning successful performance on a bigger stage to a broader audience. However, there's something else that is uniquely needed in the role of a strategist. It's called business acumen.

Ram Charan, noted business authority and adviser, defines business acumen as "linking an insightful assessment of the external business landscape with the keen awareness of how money can be made—and then executing the strategy to deliver the desired results."[32] This definition aligns with the need for strategic thinking. The difference, however, is "the keen awareness of how money can be made." This introduces a new perspective, learning about the business and applying that knowledge to job, team, or function-specific activities. Isn't this what senior leadership is supposed to do, to understand how the business makes money and set strategy, goals, and objectives that cascade down through the organization and ultimately to your role? Yes, but what's the likelihood that anyone is going to hand you a specific flowchart that pinpoints your role and specific duties needed to derive value and profitability? Remember what happened when you crossed the Rubicon. You marched into a territory called running the business. Who knows best about your role and the part of the business for which you're responsible? While senior leadership has its responsibilities, you have yours in terms of translating knowledge of the business into specific duties, priorities, choices, and decisions for you and your team.

Here is how you get a seat at the table. Build credibility, not just as someone who has functional expertise, operational know-how, and leadership success, but as a leader who understands the overall business first and the functional responsibilities second. You already have proven capability and competence. And, you have the formula for strategic leadership: It starts with seeing the big picture, crossing borders and engaging in dialogue, building partnerships, and defining the third win. Next you learn how the business makes money, apply it to your part of the business, and stay engaged in a business-wide dialogue, even if you have to invite yourself to the table. There's just one more piece.

Thinking With the Whole Brain: An Integrated Perspective

Strategic leadership is a game unlike what most experience. The good news is that you have the unique capabilities to play the game effectively and to win. Since the field of play is always shifting, someone has to be on constant lookout for the broader landscape. This is where the capability of *strategic thinking* is needed. The ability to look out to the future and work back to the present, to anticipate what's next, and determine a path forward, is critical. Unfortunately, winning is not entirely clear or within your control since the broader marketplace decides who wins. But you know that already. You've integrated the process of customer dialogue into how you and your organization do business. You know what it means to walk in your customer's shoes, even those of the paying customer, because you engage them in routine heart-to-heart discussions.

Do you implement everything your customers tell you they need? No. You use that knowledge as input into formulating a strategic direction, to understand the why behind the what. This is where another capability, *business acumen*, kicks in. Understanding the business and how the business makes money are factored into the game plan. Customers can tell you they want you to manufacture a particular product and put their label on it. Sounds good, but can you make money at it? R&D can create several products, but will customers buy them? These are the types of situations where business acumen and the sorting mechanism of strategy play a critical role.

Business Savvy: The Combination of Experience, Strategic Thinking, and Business Acumen

Looking at a different game with shifting boundaries, changing rules, and diverse ways to win is confusing, if not chaotic. Enter the need for another capability, business savvy. Being business savvy is a seasoned ability to understand the current reality and confidently move to the future. It engages both logic and emotion, a mindset created through the continuous layering of experience and insight. Business savvy is the combination of on-the-field experience and the study of game films that enables Tom Brady to change a play at the line of scrimmage for a touchdown pass. It's how Jonah Lehrer describes Michael Binger, a Stanford particle physicist and professional poker player, when Binger says that playing poker is solving a mystery, not solving a set of math problems.[33] It is a mix of strategic thinking and business acumen, and it yields a competence and confidence that neither creates on its own. Being business savvy is what gives strategic leadership its edge—part logic, part intuition. It requires deliberate reflection and creative intent, conscious thought about what you see and what it means, then filed away in unconscious memory. Business savvy is confidence and experience, faith and know-how, gut and logic all rolled into one.

Working at a strategic level is a potent combination of seeing the bigger picture, engaging with customers about what is important to them, partnering with other organizations to achieve success, and understanding how the business creates value and what it needs to do for long-term economic viability. Strategic leadership is not reserved just for senior-level executives. It is the type of leadership needed throughout the enterprise, leadership that focuses on the longer term with both the confidence and fear that nothing lasts forever. Keep in mind that the development of strategic leadership does not happen overnight. It is a deliberate process that requires a unique way of looking at the world and spending time on the right things *today* that will be critical for *tomorrow*.

Working at a Strategic Level

Self-Assessment and Action Planning Activity

A. Following are a series of statements related to elements of strategic knowledge, skills, and behaviors. Rate yourself based on the following scale:

1. Not at all
2. Rarely
3. Sometimes
4. Often
5. Continuously

To what extent do I:

Working at a strategic level	My rating
Strategic thinker	
1. Consciously take the time to reflect and ask myself how I'm thinking through an issue, what I've learned from a particular situation, what insight I've gained, and what it means for the future	
2. Think not only about what I see as important in the future but also think backwards from that point to chart a course for how to get from here to there	
3. Engage colleagues in free-wheeling discussions of ideas and future possibilities; challenge each other to think broadly and without restraint	
Walks in the customer's shoes	
4. Know who pays the bills and make sure everyone in the organization realizes that the focus on the customer is essential for economic survival	

5. Involve all levels of the organization in a systematic process to understand customer needs through ongoing customer dialogue and discussion	
6. Use the knowledge and understanding of the customer to improve processes and develop new products and services	
Business partner and strategist	
7. Partner by positioning the organization to deliver value-added services and products	
8. Learn the business partner's business and proactively provide counsel to improve the partner's performance and develop future capabilities	
9. Use knowledge and expertise from own organization to assess the potential impact of a major change/trend on the partner relationship, e.g., competitive threat or regulatory change	
Business savvy	
10. See the big picture for the business: think broadly, extrapolate from present to future trends, understand interdependencies, and develop a road map for how to reach the desired state	
11. Study market trends and use an intimate knowledge of the business and its core competencies to determine how the organization competes successfully for the long term	
12. Know how the business derives profitability, what is required for long-term economic viability, and has the battle scars to prove it	

B. Summarize your ratings in the following:

Current strengths	Current areas for improvement
1.	1.
2.	2.
3.	3.

C. Next steps:

Pick one area for improvement, just one. Look at it closely and decide what you need to do and what are the steps needed to make that improvement. If this is truly important to you, then start this process today. Create a SMART goal, determine the desired impact, the activities needed, and how you will measure your success. Make a public commitment by sharing this with three people.

SMART goal	Desired impact	Development activities	Measure of success

Chapter Summary

Mentoré leadership stage comparisons

Expertise stage	Credibility stage	Alignment & execution stage	Strategy stage
What	Who	How	Why
Track record	Image & reputation	Coaching & leading by example	Seeing the bigger picture
Knowledge & experience	Communication & influence	Decision making, prioritization & problem resolution	Insights applied to the business
Depth	Breadth	Agility	Calculated risk taking
Student of knowledge	Student of people	Student of the organization	Student of the business
Native intelligence	Emotional intelligence	Systems thinking	Strategic thinking
How smart you are	How you deliver value to others in the organization	How to maximize operational efficiencies	How to work as a partner & strategist to the business
Knowing your subject matter	Knowing your audience	Knowing your organization	Knowing your business

Taking Stock

- Strategic leadership looks up and out from the current organizational system to understand what's happening in the outside world.
- Strategic leadership asks the why behind the what: Why are we doing what we're doing?
- What differentiates strategic leadership from any other stage of development is important changes in mindset and perspective more so than just behavior.

- Leadership at this level is about the ability to think strategically, to see the big picture, regardless of where you sit in the organization. Strategic thinking

  o begins with a realization that the future begins in the present. This is the all-important element of *insight;*
  o is nonlinear in the sense that it sees more than a linear trajectory from the present to the future. At the same time, strategic thinking is not random because it builds on the current conditions and considers how these are transformed by other forces moving forward;
  o uses both logic and emotion to fuel learning and insight. What goes into the brain from observation and analytical thought pops out as flashes, epiphanies, or *aha* moments when you least expect it;
  o is visual thinking. When someone sees it, he or she can most likely illustrate it;
  o links insight with foresight, the ability to use understanding and study of past experience to predict a future pattern or trend. It is the ability to see more from less.

- One method for developing strategic thinking is through a process of anticipation, extrapolation, and translation. This means using moving beyond the current situation first to anticipate what's next, then to extrapolate to a future state, and to use that as a reference point to translate the actions required to move forward.

- Thinking strategically, like the competency of curiosity, embraces the question what if? Risk and imagination are baked into the process, they are not separate disciplines.

- It may seem like strategic thinking is brainstorming on steroids. Actually, strategic thinking is not open to all ideas. It has intent. It wants to reach a certain destination, not meander down a path of unlimited options. It's creative, but it's also logical. There is vision, and the goal is not only to see it, but to figure out how to get there. That takes commitment and confidence.

- Strategy is the framework that enables an organization to allocate resources and make choices, decisions, and trade-offs based on the vision and forward direction. Strategy is about differentiation in the marketplace, not operational efficiency.
- Strategic leadership builds upon the power of dialogue. Dialogue is a process of engagement and understanding. It is particularly important as a way to build horizontal alignment inside an organization, by crossing functional borders and ultimately connecting to the end customer.
- The value of dialogue with your customers is that it unites both of you in defining the third win, the win for your customer's customer.
- Working as a partner and strategist requires understanding the business. The expectation is that, regardless of where you sit in the organization, you are responsible for looking at the bigger picture for what makes the business profitable and how money can be made. It is this skill, the business acumen skill, which helps get you a seat at the table.
- Being business savvy creates unique capabilities. One is intuition based on a mix of past experience, lessons learned, and deliberate reflection. That creates razor-sharp know-how that lies in both conscious and unconscious thought. A second is the ability to push

$$\text{Business savvy} \int_{\text{Strategic thinking}}^{\text{Business acumen}} \textit{Experience}$$

forward with intent and confidence. Business savvy is potent, not because it is a competency reserved for senior executives, but because it makes anyone in a leadership position more impactful. It creates a win for the organization, a win for the business, and a win for the customer.

CHAPTER 6

Defying Gravity

The Unique Journey of Technical Experts into Management Positions or Not

In Chapter 1, I used the term technical expertise broadly to describe the content-specific and knowledge-based aspect of any job. Here I'm using the concept of technical experts in two broad categories. One is where the businesses themselves are technical, such as research labs, biotech organizations, civil engineering companies, IT organizations, large pharmaceutical companies, or high-tech businesses. The second is with content-driven technical specialists, such as engineers, information technologists, scientists, doctors, accountants, or researchers. These groups of professionals appreciate that leadership requires a different skill set. Two issues, however, are not always understood: (1) how someone acquires these skills, and (2) how big a role does ongoing technical competence play in leadership success? We do know from the competency research that additional technical competence alone does not create leadership success, nor will simply learning generic leadership skills give a clear road map for when, how, and where to apply these additional competencies.

The Technical Leader Conundrum

In the early 1990s, I was working with a client who was an up-and-comer in the software development business. He had asked me to design and facilitate a leadership training program for their new managers. The company began as a classic startup of three colleagues with several advanced degrees and patents under their belts working with a small team of sales and marketing professionals. At the time I began working with them they were in growth mode, hiring engineers and promoting people into technical management positions.

This was not my first time working with people with highly technical backgrounds, but it is memorable because of a series of conversations I had with the vice president of software development. A talented engineer, astute leader, and savvy business person, he was a product of a major R&D organization with a big business perspective and ample experience. His challenge was how to apply the important lessons learned to a much smaller, growing business. As we talked through his staff, he told me that he found the job of engineering manager the toughest one to staff. Why? What he told me was that the best engineers do not make the best engineering managers. They have the technical backgrounds, but they do not necessarily have the leadership skills needed for success in managerial positions. And particularly with the issue of rapid growth, he knew that many technical people had been given battlefield promotions for leadership positions that they weren't prepared for. He understood that his role was to identify, train, and develop technical managers.

This may not seem like an unusual observation—that the best engineers are not necessarily the best engineering managers. The research into leadership effectiveness continues to show that hiring the best and the brightest does not create leadership success, and that "the demonstration of nontechnical competencies continues to differentiate outstanding leadership and create the top-performing climates."[1] However, my firsthand observation is that the continuing practice of selecting the best individual contributor for a management position in technical organizations is alive and well. It seems as much an issue of practicality and expediency as opposed to an underappreciation of emotional intelligence and the skill sets related to credibility. Just hire or promote the best engineers because they have the knowledge and experience. They know what to do, so they can tell other people what to do. It is not that difficult, really. And if there is anything they need to learn, they will pick it up along the way. Their best teacher is osmosis. Their best learning environment is the school of hard knocks–trial by ordeal, 21st century style.

The VP of software development understood what he had to do. Without his insight, this situation had all the earmarks of a run and gun, pacesetting, potentially command and control environment.[2] It is the cross-country example revisited. It is as if the entire organization lines up at the starting line for the race. When the gun is fired, everyone takes off, running just as hard as they can for as long as they can until they reach the finish line. Where are the managers in this scenario? They are out there running in the field as well. They are most likely in the front of the pack since they are the best. And what is their role in the preparation and performance of their teams? Most likely, they huddled with their particular group just before the start of the race, told them to run hard, run fast, and finish strong. When the race is over, the manager looks at how each person performed, finds the people whose times are not what was expected, sees what the problems are, tells them to do better next time, and calls it a day, or most likely goes back to the office to do more work.

You may be thinking that taking the best performer and promoting that person to a manager position is not confined to the technical world. You are right about that. I have seen it firsthand in sales organizations, for example.[3] In technical environments, however, the issue of selecting leaders is trickier. In part, the issue arises out of the definition of technical leadership itself. Does it mean leadership of the technical *specialty*, or is it leadership of the *people* in that technical specialty? What makes the answer difficult is what I describe as *technical credibility*, the role technical expertise can play in terms of credibility for the technical manager. Because technical knowledge and expertise are highly valued in organizations like software engineering, they play a role in managerial success. In many types of organizations, leaders are not expected to know everything that their team members know. However, in many technical organizations, they are expected to know everything.

For technical leaders, success is not a choice of either technical expertise or leadership capability. Both are expected, but it's important to understand what the combination of these two parts would look like. It's easier to determine the level of technical expertise given an emphasis on knowledge, experience, and mastery. The tougher issue is knowing what other skills and competencies—the so-called soft skills—are needed. This is where I have used the stages and competencies in the Mentoré leadership model successfully. The concept of a base that includes both expertise and credibility makes the point that both skill sets are required. For some people, credibility, the focus on the who not the what, is a new concept.

For others, there is understanding, but there is ongoing need for practicing and reinforcing the credibility skills and mindset. Such is the process for leadership development.

To think that moving into technical leadership positions is a linear process facilitated by adopting a laundry list of leadership behaviors is simplistic. Moving into those positions is still an evolutionary process. Because the role of technical expertise is critical to success in technical organizations, the road to strategic leadership positions, whether as managers of people or as high-level individual contributors, is a series of progressions. While the stages align to the Mentoré model, the mesh of technical and nontechnical skills requires a somewhat different development process, one in which both elements are needed to acclimate and ascend into positions that have a greater impact on organizational success.

The Types of Technical Leadership Positions

Earlier I proposed what I see as the skill and competency requirements for a subject matter expert, an SME. My experience, similar to that in the Bell Labs study, is that both technical mastery and credibility are needed for SME success.[4] It is one thing to have the knowledge and experience; it is another thing to have the knowledge and experience plus the value others derive from your performance. It is what Goleman describes as "techies with passion and intuition."[5] I call them "right-brain engineers." The reason for restating this point is to clarify that the rites of passage for technical leaders, similar to that of their nontechnical counterparts, must be through these first two stages. It is the grounding needed to move forward in your career.

Beyond the credibility stage in technical organizations, however, it is not unusual to see the road for career choice fork in two directions:

1. *The managerial track*
   The managerial track is similar to what you might except in any organization, moving from individual contributor, to a team lead, then to supervisor, manager, director, and executive positions. Obviously, organizations have different ways to slice these jobs. Typically,

each movement up leads to a broader scope of responsibilities across the functional organization and across the business.

The managerial track for a technical professional follows the same stage movement through the Mentoré model:

a. Grounding yourself in technical mastery in the expertise stage.
b. Increasing your personal value to the organization and potentially attaining SME status through the credibility stage.
c. Crossing into the business and managing through others in the alignment and execution stage.
d. Taking a broader role for running the business in the strategy stage.

However, we know that the picture is colored by how much technical expertise is required as one moves into and through the management ranks. In those organizations where the best performers are promoted into management positions, one sees a high level of technical expertise and emphasis on technical credibility for senior leaders. However, in those cases, it is hard to know if that is by intent or default. It is not always clear how much thought and planning are given to the definition of job success for mid- to senior-level management positions. Hopefully, these ranks are filled with leaders who have the nontechnical competencies because we know that these skills and behaviors contribute to outstanding performance.[6]

2. *The technical track*

The second career path is for the technical professionals who want to spend their careers more deeply involved in their technical specialties as opposed to managing others. Many organizations, especially those in technical fields, have such a career ladder.[7] For the professional moving up the technical ladder, we know that credibility and emotional intelligence are critical. However, the argument *for* emotional intelligence is not an argument *against* more technical expertise. The issue of what and how much technical expertise is needed should be based on what the business requires. This happens by drilling down on core competencies and competitive differentiation to define the technical skills and competencies that the business requires, which subsequently determines what individual technical capabilities to cultivate.

Technical Track Professionals and Organizational Capacity

Technical track professionals also have responsibilities in the two higher-level stages, alignment and execution and strategy. Here the issue is a familiar one of building organization capacity. There is the skill set needed to work through others that, for technical professionals, most often occurs when they lead or join major cross-functional initiatives or projects. The competencies related to influence without formal authority, getting buy in, and selling ideas across an organization are all important. So is the competency for leading by example. However, without the responsibility of direct reports, there is less formal emphasis on talent development. The exception here is the role the technical professional can play as a teacher for his or her technical specialty. For the technical track professional, the roll-up of these competencies is the knowledge and insight of what it takes to execute through others. It's the seasoning that the technical professionals develop for broad-based implementation, even though they are not formally responsible on a daily basis for managing others.

There are, however, two other expectations for technical track professionals in terms of building capacity. One is the expectation of broadening their personal experience through cross-functional initiatives. This could be realized by applying current knowledge to new situations, acquiring new knowledge, or working in completely new areas of the organization. In other words, there is an expected expansion of the technical base, sometimes opportunistic, but always with the intent to build a personal reservoir of applied knowledge and experience.

A second expectation is an understanding of the business and how technical expertise plays a role in building additional capability. I would argue that as technical track professionals move into the higher stages of the organization, they are expected to acquire a broader understanding of the business context in which they work. For example, I worked with a large client who had recently contracted out his entire manufacturing operations. I was talking to a director for a design engineering group and asked him what his team did. He told me a classic before-and-after story. Before contract manufacturing, their job was to create product prototypes. After contract manufacturing, there job was to figure out how to take a dollar out of the manufacturing costs. What this illustrates is the application of technical expertise to the *business*, not simply expanding technical knowledge. He said it was a whole new experience for both him and the team.

If one of the outcomes of strategic leadership is becoming business savvy, then what does this look like for the technical track professionals? It's tempting to say that it is tech savvy, but it seems that expression is already taken, generally used to mean that someone is knowledgeable about how technology works. The technical track professionals I'm describing understand the

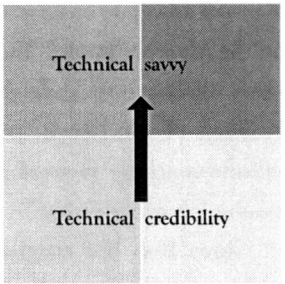

business and the broad implications of their experience. Once they cross into the higher stages of leadership development, their mission is becoming *technical savvy*, the integration of broad-based technical expertise with business acumen, the understanding of the business, and how the business makes money. These individuals are technical resources up and down the organization who have the skills and experience to work as strategists to the business, not just as high-level functional specialists.

Making the Shift

The process for leadership development, like so many advancements in education and science in the past 50 years, continues to evolve. Today we have a better understanding of how to train and develop leaders based on behaviors that are indicative of the knowledge, skills, traits, and characteristics of the best. We see a growing interest in talent development and the implications for leadership and leadership development. We study the impact of emotional intelligence and being business savvy on leadership effectiveness. And we build on the firsthand observations of practitioners in the field who work to develop leaders at a ground level every day.

One such practitioner is Dr. Robert Hewes. Bob is a senior partner at Camden Consulting Group, an executive coaching and leadership development firm in Boston. He is also one of the best leadership coaches I know. Bob holds a doctorate in engineering science from Harvard University, and master of science and bachelor of science degrees from University of New Hampshire. The way I see it is that a PhD and executive coach combination yields either a right-brain engineer, a left-brain coach, or a whole-brain expert; take your pick. Since 2010, he and I have worked together to create and facilitate a leadership development program based on the Mentoré model. The target population is technical experts who are in or moving into leadership roles. The nine-month program is a combination of workshops, peer group interactions, assessments, and one-on-one coaching focused on the application of leadership behaviors for on-the-job effectiveness.[8]

Since Bob has coached many technical professionals and people within technical organizations, he has a perspective on how the concept of leader evolution resonates with his clients. In interviewing Bob for this book, I asked him what he thinks is the most important insight. The way he often describes the leadership development process based on the Mentoré model is about *making the shift*. Bob describes how some individuals tend to bump up against a ceiling created by their technical expertise. To understand that they can expand their individual effectiveness by looking at credibility is a way to eliminate that barrier. "When I talk about making the shift from expertise to credibility," Bob describes, "everyone gets this one, literally everyone." Part of the issue, he explains, is that some people miss the fact that credibility plays a role in their ability to manage, lead, and execute effectively. Bob explains that it is not a matter of doing it alone or being the smartest in the room anymore that makes a difference. It is about making *the shift*, from knowing the answer to getting people to believe in you. The insight that people begin to appreciate is that "*who* I'm working with is as important as *what* I'm working on."[9]

Another important element that Bob describes is having a framework, a road map that enables leaders to understand where they are in terms of their development and where they are headed. Bob adds, "The notion of growth is not the same as making a shift. People know that there's something (they need to do) differently." What this means is that it takes a deliberate change in perspective and mindset to grasp what is needed, not just adopting a single skill like delegation or giving feedback or running an effective meeting. The difference is that the shift requires a "constellation of competencies and knowing where to land." In the case of credibility, for example, it is how to involve others. As people start to understand why that's important, they continue to use that insight. As Bob describes, "Once you cross over, you never go back."[10]

Making a Choice

A final point that Dr. Hewes makes is that technical professionals need to make a choice about making the shift. With a model of the stages in leader evolution, they can clearly see the expectations and make a decision about what are their interests and where they want to head in their careers. On this point, he is emphatic, "I believe that this should be a choice." In other words, not everyone in a technical field should aspire for a management position.[11] Making the shift is also about making a choice.

Chapter Summary

Taking Stock

- Technical professions and technical organizations place a high value on knowledge and experience, and this creates a unique challenge for leadership selection.
- What makes technical leadership positions unique is the extent to which credibility is attached to technical expertise. This *technical credibility* factor casts a big shadow and appears to loom large in the leadership selection process.
- Nonetheless, the research into leadership effectiveness is compelling: Emotional intelligence is required, even in technical environments. It seems that the rites of passage for what Goleman describes as "techies with passion and intuition" and I describe as "right-brain engineers" are through the credibility stage of the Mentoré model.[12]
- Technical organizations often create a dual career path with management and nonmanagement or technical professional tracks.

    - The management track is similar to what you would expect to see in nontechnical organizations: Alignment and

execution focus on building capacity through team and
team member development; strategic leadership focuses on
developing a broader knowledge of the business.

- The technical professional track, however, is different.
The expectation of building organizational capacity is
through increased capability of the technical professional.
This happens by flying solo. However, it is also built in
the context of working on cross-functional or large-scale
change initiatives where technical depth and breadth are
mutually beneficial outcomes for the individual and the
business. There is also the expectation for the technical
professional to build capacity by teaching others. From
the strategic leadership perspective, the expectation is one
of becoming *technical savvy*, a combination of technical
experience and business acumen. In other words, it's the
application of the technical knowledge to how the *business*
is successful now and moving forward.

- Making the shift means a change in mindset, moving from
technical expertise to credibility, from "what I'm working
on, to who I'm working with." Making the shift also refers to
adopting a constellation of competencies as opposed to a skill-
by-skill approach to leadership development.

CHAPTER 7

Coda

As Mr. Swofford, my eighth grade and high-school math teacher, would say, "It's time to put away your book, take out paper and pencil, and answer a few questions." I still remember what it was like when I heard those words. You could cut the dread in the room with a knife. You see, Mr. Swofford never told us in advance when we were having a test—not once in five years. He was a brilliant and wonderful man, an incredible teacher, and he taught the value of continuously preparing to end up in the right place.

The mentoré leadership competency model

Alignment and execution	Strategy
Credibility	Expertise

If you don't know where you are going, you'll end up someplace else.
Lawrence Peter Berra

Now it is your turn. Think about where you are and where you are headed by answering these questions:

1. Who owns your development as a leader? Provide a rationale.
2. Where are you right now in your own leadership evolution? Depending on where you are, what is or has been the hardest shift or transition? Say more.
3. To what extent are you demonstrating the behaviors, thought process, and perspective that define success in your particular development stage and position? Give three examples.
4. To what extent are you operating at the right level, meaning that you are maximizing your ability to impact and effectively lead your team, your organization, and your part of the business? What helps you in this pursuit? What are the obstacles that you face?

5. If you are not where you need to be, what are the steps needed to move you in the right direction? Create a SMART goal with the action steps that support it. Include the desired impact and measures of success.

For extra credit:

What will you do moving forward that will enable you to continuously get smarter, particularly as it relates to your effectiveness as a leader? Be specific.

OK, pencils down. Now that you have had an opportunity to think through these questions, let us go back and review the major concepts together. For starters, the basic premise throughout this discussion is the focus on leadership behavior—how, when, where, and why changes in behavior are needed. At some points it is about acquiring new behaviors; at other times, it is about letting go. We know that some behaviors are easily trained, like how to run an effective meeting; some have to be developed over time, like elevating team performance; and some that are tied closer to aptitude and personality characteristics, like moral courage, are not easily trained and are tougher to develop. Such differences reflect the amount of effort that you need to acquire and use these behaviors effectively. Your *development* as a leader, therefore, requires intent, practice, application, and feedback. You own your professional development. Even if you have an organization or manager that believes in you, you still must drive the process.

> *Leaders are visionaries with a poorly developed sense of fear and no concept of the odds against them.*
> Robert Jarvick

Moving into leadership positions is the ability to defy gravity. This applies across the board, not just to those individuals in technical professions. The years of schooling and value placed on being smart keep us grounded, or so we think. There is a sense of security and control that comes with expertise. But then there's the need to understand people and work through others who may not share the same standards, let alone interests, that we have. Add in the calculus of change in today's world, and for good measure, throw in the uncertainty about the future. And what is often the tendency? To let gravity take over and pull us back into expertise, which means finding the answer, being right, and retreating to an area where we feel we are in control. Effective leadership is the ability to demonstrate confidence and move forward in a less-than-button-downed world. Leadership is like running a marathon; it's a race against slowing down.[1]

Effective leadership development is not simply trying to learn a list of behaviors on a competency-by-competency basis. Such a list encapsulates a desired skill set, but it does not provide a context or a way to make these skills stick. In the words of Dr. Hewes, the story is better told by the need to *make the shift*, to look at constellations rather than individual behaviors. It is better to understand how certain behaviors and thought processes work together, then practice and apply them, and learn from the experience. It's movement into a different stage with a different focus, mindset, and skills. It is assimilation followed by accommodation over time.

Thinking About Thinking

If leadership development is to succeed, a change in thinking and perspective must also accompany certain critical changes in behavior. For example, moving into the alignment and execution stage requires developing the skill set to accomplish work through others, but it also requires a conscious thought process for letting go certain responsibilities by delegating and developing the team's capability. Moving into a strategic leadership position requires a big picture and future perspective as well as the skills associated with creating partnerships or deploying strategy.

The term metacognition, often described as thinking about thinking, is a principle discussed in the educational and psychological fields about an individual's capability to learn.[2] We have discussed how metacognition is also applicable for leadership, particularly as someone enters a new stage of development. The change in mindset is the euphemistic paradigm shift. All this sounds like a riddle, thinking about thinking and *deliberate reflection*. But it is an important riddle. A change in thought process changes what you see, how you think through a situation, and how you make judgments and decisions.

Throughout the evolution of leadership, metacognition is important for several reasons:

- It unleashes the transformative power of discernment and curiosity, two of the original building blocks needed for expertise. Discernment is the thought-provoking side, the never-ending need to understand what and why. Curiosity is the itch, the playful side that also likes why but dares ask what if, even as the doors are closing on the situation or decision. What is important is how they evolve together throughout the leadership development process, from analytical thinking and needing to understand what's inside the box, to understanding people and building credibility, to systems thinking and the press-box view needed for organizational alignment, to strategic thinking, seeing the bigger picture, engaging both risk taking and imagination in the process, and blowing up the box and seeing the same elements in vastly different ways for different outcomes in the future. It may not qualify as chaos theory, but it's a close approximation.
- Metacognition speaks to the importance of learning, the ability to look beyond the obvious, and question the assumptions that underlie an action or decision.[3]
- It pushes toward mastery and accepts that it's always possible to get better.
- It opens the door to think broadly and make informed judgments, to learn from both failure and success.
- It keeps you in shape mentally and emotionally. It's as Lehrer describes—"the conscious thought process that regulates emotions."[4]
- Metacognition enables you to make better decisions. Lehrer continues:

Whenever you make a decision, be aware of the kind of decision you are making and the kind of that process it requires. It doesn't matter if you're choosing between wide receivers or political candidates. You might be playing poker or assessing the results of a television focus group. The best way to make sure that you are using your brain properly is to study your brain at work, to listen to the argument inside your head. Why is thinking about thinking so important? First, it helps you steer clear of stupid errors . . . . There is no secret recipe for decision-making. There is only vigilance, the commitment to avoiding those errors that can be avoided. Of course, even the most attentive and self-aware minds will still make mistakes. Tom Brady, after the perfect season of 2008, played poorly in the Super Bowl . . . . But the best decision makers don't despair. Instead, they become students of error, determined to learn from what went wrong.[5]

- Metacognition is the ability to convert insight into foresight, to see more from less, to deconstruct the current reality into pixels that are reconstructed into a vision of the future and a path for moving forward.

How metacognition relates to effective leadership is yet again the need to engage the whole brain in the development process. Acquiring, eliminating, and changing behavior are accompanied by the thought process for what you do, how you do it, and why you do it. This is not to say that every action requires deliberate reflection before acting. It is, however, to suggest that the change sticks because the thought process and behavior constantly talk to each other. The greater the understanding that underlies the behavior, the greater the opportunity to move the behavior and thinking process in the same direction.

What makes a great leader is a repertoire of critical behaviors and thought processes with the flexibility to engage with people, tasks, and business, all in the pursuit of organizational success. On a personal level, success is the use of the right behavior at the right time for the right purpose for a desired outcome.

Some people are predisposed to leadership, the so-called natural leaders who have the genetic wiring to be successful. However, the vast majority of effective leaders are made. Since the mid-20th century, the understanding of leadership success has been put under an electron microscope to isolate effective behaviors, skill sets, and competencies. And with the studies of researchers like Goleman,[6] Davidson,[7] and Lehrer,[8] there is increasing interest in the relationship of brain science with types of intelligence and leadership effectiveness. As this understanding increases, the process for developing effective leaders will continue to expand into new territory.

For now, the need for effective leadership could not be greater. The bombardment of information, the technological changes in communication that are most likely rewiring our brains, the fact that many people lose control of their schedules the minute they walk into their offices, the sheer volume of distractions—all of these conditions speak to the need to step up into leadership roles with or without the formal titles. But the biggest challenge I see is the one that exists inside your head. *It's not about being smart, it's about getting smart.* It also means being clever and becoming savvy. It is not just that you are knowledgeable, it is that you understand what makes people tick, organizations effective, and the business profitable.

The evolution of successful leadership is the ability to lead change and feel comfortable in not having all the answers, much less the right answer. The proliferation of responsibilities inside a highly connected yet fragmented world means that the need to influence the way that others think and feel to the point they take responsible and decisive action will only intensify. The more strategic the leadership, the broader your personal impact and the greater the value you bring to organizational success.

Notes

Preface

1. Leeson (2010).
2. Amato (2013).
3. Amato (2013).
4. Goleman (1998).

Chapter 1

1. Kotter (1999).
2. Yukl (2012).
3. Carlyle (2011). Carlyle's original essay was published on May 5, 1840.
4. Allport (1937).
5. *Leadership Theories—In Chronological Order*. Retrieved February 18, 2014, from http://www.leadership-central.com/leadership-theories.html).
6. *Leadership Theories* (2014).
7. *Leadership Theories* (2014).
8. *Leadership Theories* (2014).
9. Blake and Mouton (1972).
10. Hersey and Blanchard (2012).
11. Bass (2006).
12. Burns (1985).
13. McClelland (1973).
14. Boyatzis (1982).
15. Spencer (1993).
16. Goleman (1995).
17. McClelland (1973).
18. Goleman (2005).
19. Knowles (1984).
20. Crain (1985), pp. 118–136.
21. Crain (1985).
22. Crain (1985).
23. Herzberg (1959).
24. Maslow (1954).
25. David McClelland, often described as the founder of this movement, created a bit of a stir with a 1973 paper in which he said that competence, not IQ, was a better predictor of job success. See McClelland (1973).

26. McClelland (1973).
27. Mentoré is the name of my consulting practice. Mentoré is Italian for "mentor."
28. Blake and Mouton (1972); Hersey and Blanchard (2012).
29. This refers to the body of work from the research of Boyatzis (1982), Spencer (1993), and Goleman (1995).
30. Burns (1985); Bass (2006).
31. The title that Jay Conger uses for his article in *Harvard Business Review* (1998).
32. Charan (2006).

Chapter 2

1. Sir Francis Bacon was said to have made this statement. See http://en.wikipedia.org/wiki/Scientia_potentia_est. Some also know this as their high-school motto.
2. Maslow (1954).
3. Herzberg (1959).
4. McClelland (1961); McClelland (1987).
5. McClelland and Burnham (2003).
6. McClelland (1987).
7. McClelland (1987).
8. Gardner (1983).
9. Gardner (1983), p. xv.
10. Gardner (2008), p. xv.
11. Gardner (2008), pp. xiii–xv.
12. Argyris and Shon (1974).
13. Argyris and Shon (1974).
14. Pink (2005).
15. Pink (2005), pp. 51–52.
16. Pink (2005), pp. 61–65.
17. For the record, I made it, crossed the finish line in 3:05, and ended my short marathon career on a high note.
18. One of the important characteristics Collins describes of the Level 5 leaders in "good to great" companies is their will. He comments, "these leaders are fanatically driven, infected with an incurable need to produce sustained *results*. . . . Level 5 leaders display workmanlike diligence—more plow horse than show horse." Collins (2001), p. 39. I would add that at the stage of expertise, leaders are "plow horses in training."
19. Argyris and Shon (1974).
20. Gardner (2008).

21. Pink (2005).
22. The "Odd Couple" is a reference to the Neil Simon Broadway play that opened in 1965 and later became both a movie and television series. It is a story of how two divorced men, Felix Unger who is neat and tidy, and Oscar Madison who is casual and sloppy, live together in a New York apartment.
23. Carol Dweck uses a similar line of reasoning in her description of mastery in which she describes the difference between a fixed mindset and growth mindset. Additional information can be found in Pink (2009), pp. 118–120, pp. 199–200; Dweck (1999).
24. According to the American Institute of CPAs, "All CPA candidates must pass the Uniform CPA Examination to qualify for a CPA certificate and license (i.e., permit to practice) to practice public accounting." From their website http://www.aicpa.org/BECOMEACPA/LICENSURE/Pages/default.aspx
25. Examples of HR certifications and their requirements can be found on the HR Certification website: http://www.hrci.org/our-programs/what-is-hr-certification
26. Pink (2009), p. 109.
27. Pink (2009), pp. 124–125.
28. Pink (2009), pp. 118–120; Dweck (1999).
29. Pink (2009), pp. 121–122.
30. Colvin (2010), pp. 71–72.

Chapter 3

1. Goleman (1998).
2. Goleman (1998), pp. 15–17.
3. Goleman (1998).
4. Boyatzis (1982).
5. Spencer (1993).
6. Zenger and Folkman (2002), p. 88.
7. Goleman (1998), pp. 33–38.
8. Goleman (1998), pp. 133–136.
9. Conger (1998).
10. Bacon (2011), p. 114.
11. Bennis (1989).
12. Kouses and Posner (2007).
13. Covey (1989).
14. Zenger (2002), pp. 196–197.
15. Peters and Waterman (1982).
16. Uzzi and Dunlap (December, 2005).
17. Zenger (2002), pp. 196–197.

18. Drucker (2001), p. 261.
19. Drucker (2001), pp. 261–267.
20. Drucker (2001), p. 267.
21. I created *FLÉR* as an acronym to use with clients in workshops: focus, listen, engage, restate.
22. Pink (2005), p. 115.
23. I took the liberty of adding an accent to Éngage.
24. Covey (1989).
25. Bacon (2011), p. 70. In this section, Bacon quotes the work of Robert Cialdini.
26. Bacon (2011), p. 70.
27. Pink (2012) pp. 20–21.
28. Pink (2012), pp. 28–29.
29. Cialdini (1993).
30. Bacon (2011).
31. Goleman (1998).
32. Goleman (1998), pp. 133–134.
33. Mehrabian (1971).
34. Goleman (1998), pp. 145–146.
35. Covey (1989).
36. Conger (1993).
37. This is the Merriam-Webster definition for a "suck up": http://www.merriam-webster.com/dictionary/suck-up
38. Peter(1969).
39. Goleman (1998), p. 42.
40. Zenger (2002).
41. Kelley (1993).
42. Zenger (2002), p. 183.
43. Kelley (1993).
44. Kelley (1993).

Chapter 4

1. "Iacta alia est" is Latin for the "die is cast." For more information, consult the following: http://en.wikipedia.org/wiki/Alea_iacta_est
2. Bierman (2013).
3. Bolman and Deal (2008), p. 269.
4. Bolman and Deal (2008).
5. Bolman and Deal (2008).
6. Collins (2001). Collins summarizes the findings on pp. 12–13. The expressions and characterization in quotes are the author's own descriptions.

7. Collins (2001).
8. Collins (2001).
9. Collins (2001), p. 7.
10. Bossidy and Charan (2002), pp. 98–99.
11. Spreier et al. (2006).
12. Spreier et al. (2006).
13. Aronson (2014).
14. Smith (2001).
15. Robbins and Judge (2011), p. 489.
16. PMI Standards Committee (2010).
17. Phillips (1983).
18. Marshak. (2005).
19. Kotter (2011).
20. The movie *Apollo 13*, directed by Ron Howard, came out in 1995. Although it does not appear to have been a direct quote at the actual time of the mission, the line was given to the character Gene Kranz, the NASA flight director. For more information, consult the webpage: http://www.spaceacts.com/notanoption.htm
21. Kotter (1995).
22. Conner (1993). Conner was the first to use the term "burning platform" to refer to the needs that organizations had to deal with the introduction of new technology.
23. Kotter (2008), p. 15.
24. Collins (2011), p. 24.
25. In Kotter (2008), p. 13, Kotter describes the problems inherent with under-communication, particularly with the people who need to buy in.
26. Piaget identified assimilation and accommodation as two important processes in the field of cognitive development. According to Piaget, assimilation uses the same "schema" or thought process to integrate new information. In accommodation, the "schema" changes in order to "accommodate" a different way of thinking. There are numerous sources about Piaget as well as the number of books that he wrote. For more information consult Mussen, *Handbook of Child Psychology* (1983).
27. Kotter (2008).
28. Doyle and Smith (2001); Blake and Mouton (1972); Hersey and Blanchard (2012).
29. Doyle and Smith (2001).
30. Spreier et al. (2006).
31. Patterson (2009).
32. Buckingham (2001).
33. Buckingham (2001), pp. 25–29.

34. There are several tools available for this purpose, such as the Strengths Finder assessment developed by the Gallup organization.

35. Buckingham (2001).

36. There are several references to the Carolina-Duke rivalry. Go to the following webpage for more information: http://espn.go.com/endofcentury/s/other/bestrivalries.html

37. Blythe (2006).

38. Colvin (2010). Colvin bases his argument on research conducted by Ericsson (1993), "The Role of Deliberate Practice in the Acquisition of Expert Performance."

39. Colvin (2010), p. 63.

40. Colvin (2010), pp. 66–71.

41. Colvin (2010), pp. 84–104.

42. Colvin (2010), pp. 126–144.

43. Goleman (1998), pp. 108–109. Goleman describes the concept of presence as being self-aware and in the moment. I have tied this concept with what it takes to lead by example.

44. Belasco and Stayer (1993).

45. Belasco and Stayer (1993), pp. 35–37.

46. Collins (2001).

Chapter 5

1. The "2000 year old man" is a comedy routine created by Carl Reiner and Mel Brooks. The several routines were made into an album originally released in 1960 as World-Pacific #1401. It was reissued as Capitol #1529 in 1961. More recently, see *Carl Reiner & Mel Brooks: The Complete 2000 Year Old Man* (Los Angeles, CA: Rhino Records), 1994. The sketch with Phil is on disc 4.

2. Liedtka (1998).

3. Mintzberg (1994).

4. Nasi (1991).

5. Hamel and Prahalad (1994).

6. Liedtka (1998), p. 121.

7. Liedtka (1998).

8. Liedtka (1998), p. 122.

9. Sanders (1998).

10. Neil Armstrong's famous quote when he landed on the moon is, "This is one small step for a man, one giant leap for mankind." There is a debate whether "a" was actually part of his quote. For more information, see http://www.ndtv.com/: http://www.ndtv.com/article/world/is-neil-armstrong-s-famous-moon-landing-quote-really-a-misquote-375900

11. Sanders (1998), pp. 58–59. The figure, known as the Lorenz attractor, is called the butterfly effect because of its shape. Also, Lorenz described the phenomenon in a paper delivered to the American Association for the Advancement of Science, December 29, 1972, entitled, *Predictability: Does the Flap of a Butterfly's Wings in Brazil Set Off a Tornado in Texas?*
12. Sanders (1998).
13. Sanders (1998). p. 93.
14. Sanders (1998).
15. Sanders (1998), p. 52.
16. Sanders (1998), p. 60.
17. Gladwell (2005). The phrase "*the power of thinking without thinking*" is part of the book title for *Blink.*
18. Gladwell (2005), pp. 176–184.
19. Definition taken from whatis.com. The url is http://whatis.techtarget.com/definition/extrapolation-and-interpolation
20. Vogelstein (2013).
21. Liedtka (1998).
22. Horwath, (2011), p. 5.
23. Horwath, (2011), pp. 17–19.
24. Horwath (2011), pp. 54–55.
25. Horwath (2011), p. 28.
26. Welch (2005), pp. 165–188.
27. Porter (1996).
28. Porter (1996).
29. Yankelovich (1999).
30. Yankelovich (1999), p. 23.
31. Smith (2001), p. 9.
32. Charan (2006).
33. Lehrer (2009), pp. 230–23.

Chapter 6

1. Goleman (2013), pp. 234–235. A study conducted by the Hay Group on a sample of 404 leaders analyzed the relationship of nontechnical (EI) competencies, organizational climate, and leadership styles. According to Goleman, the study supports the "same hard case for the soft skills" (p. 235).
2. These observations are similar to the comparisons made in Sprier (2006) and Goleman (2013, p. 291, footnote 4) regarding the studies of high achievers who are promoted into leadership positions.
3. Bolden (2011) also reports a similar finding in sales organizations.
4. Kelley (1993).

5. Goleman (1998), p. 45.

6. Spencer (1993), Boyatzis (1982), and Goleman (1998).

7. Tobin (2012).

8. Hewes and Patterson (2012).

9. Interview with Dr. Robert Hewes, April 15, 2014.

10. Hewes (2014). The point made here is that once a person adopts a broader perspective, in this case thinking about the "who," you begin to understand the importance of credibility and the need to understand the people around you. It becomes a conscious part of your thinking, and you "never go back" to thinking that expertise alone is enough to build credibility.

11. Hewes (2014).

12. Goleman (1998), p. 45.

Chapter 7

1. It is my recollection that Bill Rogers made this statement about running the marathon; however, I have not been able to verify that he actually said this.

2. Flavel (1979).

3. Argyris (1974). This is the concept of double-loop learning that Argyris describes.

4. Lehrer (2009).

5. Lehrer (2009).

6. Goleman (2006).

7. Davidson (2012).

8. Lehrer (2009).

References

Alea Iacta Est. n.d. en.wikipedia.org: http://en.wikipedia.org/wiki/Alea_iacta_ est, (February 3, 2014).

Allport, G. 1937. *Personality: A Psychological Interpretation.* New York, NY: Holt, Rinehart, & Winston.

Amato, N. 2013. "Top 20 Companies for Leadership Development." CGMA. http://www.cgma.org/magazine/news/pages/20138765.aspx, (September 23, 2013).

Argyris, C., and Schon, D. 1974. *Theory in Practice: Increasing Professional Effectiveness.* San Francisco. CA: Jossey-Bass.

Aronson, D. 2014. "Overview of Systems Thinking." Thinking. http://resources21. org/cl/files/project264_5674/OverviewSTarticle.pdf, (February 12, 2014).

Bacon, T. 2011. *The Elements of Power.* New York, NY: Amacom.

Bacon, T. 2012. *Elements of Influence.* New York, NY: Amacom.

Bass, B. 1985. *Leadership and Performance.* New York, NY: Free Press.

Bass, B. 2006. *Transformational Leadership.* 2nd ed. Mahwah, NJ: Lawrence Erlbaum Associates.

Belasco, J. 1993. *The Flight of the Buffalo.* New York, NY: Business Plus.

Bennis, W. 1989. *On Becoming a Leader.* Reading, MA: Addison-Wesley Publishing Company.

Bierman, B. 2013. "Q&A: Steadicam Inventor and Rocky Cinematographer Garrett Brown." *Philadelphia City Paper.* http://citypaper.net/: http://citypaper.net/article.php?Q-A-Steadicam-inventor-and-Rocky-cinematographer-Garrett-Brown-12242, (April 7, 2014).

Blake, R. 1972. *The Managerial Grid: Key Orientations for Achieving Production Through People.* 17th ed. Houston, TX: Gulf Publishing Company.

Blythe, W. 2006. *To Hate Like This is to be Happy Forever.* New York, NY: HarperCollins.

Bolden, T. 2011. "Do Top Salespeople Make Great Sales Leaders?" The Leader's Brand. http://theleadersbrand.com/2011/12/13/from-salesperson-to-sales leader, (April 20, 2014).

Bolman, L. 2008. *Reframing Organizations.* 4th ed. San Francisco, CA: Jossey-Bass

Bossidy, L. 2002. *Execution.* New York, NY: Crown Business.

Boyatzis, R. 1982. *The Competent Manager: A Model for Effective Performance.* New York, NY: John Wiley and Sons.

Carlyle, T. 2011. *On Heroes, Hero Worship, and the Heroic in History.* Seattle, WA CreateSpace Independent Publishing Platform.

Charan, R. 2006. "Sharpening Your Business Acumen." http://www.strategy-business.com/article/06106?pg=all. Strategy+Business.

Cialdini, R. 1993. *Influence: The Psychology of Persuasion.* New York, NY: William Morrow.

Collins, J. 2001. *Good to Great.* New York, NY: HarperCollins.

Collins, J. 2011. *Great by Choice.* New York, NY: HarperCollins.

Colvin, G. 2010. *Talent is Overrated.* New York, NY: Portfolio.

Committee, P.S. 2010. *A Guide to the Project Management Body of Knowledge (PMBOK Guide).* Newtown Square, PA: Project Management Institute.

Conger, J. 1998. *The Art of Persuasion.* Boston, MA: Harvard Business Review. http://hbr.org/

Conner, D. 1993. *Managing at Speed of Change.* New York, NY: Random House.

Covey, S. 1989. *The 7 Habits of Highly Effective People.* New York, NY: Fireside.

Davidson, R. 2013. *The Emotional Life of your Brain.* New York, NY: Penguin Group.

Doyle, M.E. 2001. "Classical Leadership." Infed. http://www.infed.org/leadership/traditional_leadership.htm

Drucker, P. 1986. *Managing for Results.* New York, NY: Harper.

Drucker, P. 2001. The *Essential Drucker.* New York, NY: Harper.

Dweck, C. 1999. *Self Theories: Their Role in Motivation, Personality, and Development.* Philadelphia, PA: Psychology Press.

Dyer, J.E. 2011. *The Innovators DNA.* Boston, MA: Harvard Business Review Press.

Ericsson, A.E. 1993. "The Role of Deliberate Practice in the Acquisition of Expert Performance." *Psychological Review*, 100(3), 363–406.

Flavell, J. 1979. "Metacognition and Cognitive Monitoring: A New Area of Cognitive-Development inquiry." *American Psychologist* 34(10), 906–911.

Gardner, H. 1983. *Frames of Mind: The Theory of Multiple Intelligences.* New York, NY: Basic Books.

Gardner, H. 2008. *5 Minds of the Future.* Boston, MA: Harvard Business Press.

Gladwell, M. 2005. *Blink.* New York, NY: Little, Brown and Company.

Gladwell, M. 2005. *Blink: The Power of Thinking Without Thinking.* New York, NY: Little Brown and Company.

Goleman, D. 1998. *Working with Emotional Intelligence.* New York, NY: Bantam Books.

Goleman, D. 2005. *Emotional Intelligence.* 10th ed. New York, NY: Bantam Books.

Goleman, D. 2006. *Social Intelligence: The New Science of Human Relationships.* New York, NY: Bantam Books.

Goleman, D. 2013. *Focus*. New York, NY: HarperCollins.

Hamel, G. 1994. *Competing for the Future*. Boston, MA: Harvard School Press.

Hersey, P. 2012. *Management of Organizational Behavior: Leading Human Resources*. 10th ed. Upper Saddle River, NJ: Prentice Hall.

Herzberg, T. 1959. *The Motivation to Work*. New York, NY: Wiley.

Hewes, R. 2014. *Senior Partner*. Camden Consulting Group (April 15, A. Patterson, Interviewer).

Hewes, R.P., and Patterson, A.M. 2012. "A Three-Pronged Approach to Leadership Development." *Association for Talent Development*, pp. 52–55.

Horwath, R. 2011. *Deep Dive*. Austin, TX: Greenleaf Book Group Press.

Howard, R. (Director) 1995. *Apollo 13* [Motion Picture].

Kelley, R., and J. Caplan. 1993. "How Bell Labs Creates Star Performers." *Harvard Business Review*. http://hbr.org/1993/07/how-bell-labs-creates-star-performers/ar/1

Knowles, M. 1984. *The Adult Learner: A Neglected Species*. 3rd ed. Houston, TX: Gulf Publishing.

Kotter, J. 1995. "Leading Change Why Transformation Efforts Fail." *Harvard Business Review*. http://hbr.org/2007/01/leading-change-why-transformation-efforts-fail/ar/1

Kotter, J. 1999. *What Leaders Really Do*. Boston, MA: Harvard Business Press.

Kotter, J. 2008. *A Sense of Urgency*. Boston, MA: Harvard Business Press.

Kotter, J. 2011, July, 2012. "Change Management vs. Change Leadership—What's the Difference?" Forbes http://www.forbes.com/sites/johnkotter/2011/07/12/change-management-vs-change-leadership-whats-the-difference

Kouzes, J.A. 2007. *The Leadership Challenge*. 4th Ed. San Francisco, CA: Jossey Bass.

Leeson, P. 2010. "Justice, Medieval Style." Boston: Today's Globe. http://www.boston.com/bostonglobe/ideas/articles/2010/01/31/justice_medieval_style, (January 31, 2014).

Lehrer, J. 2009. *How We Decide*. Boston, MA: Houghton Mifflin Harcourt.

Lehrer, J. 2012. *Imagine: How Creativity Works*. Boston, MA: Houghton, Mifflin, Harcourt.

Liedtka, J. 1998. "Strategic Thinking: Can it be Taught?" *Long Range Planning*, 31, no. 1, pp. 120–29.

Lorenz, E. 1993. *The Essence of Chaos*. Seattle, WA: University of Washington Press.

Marshak, R. 2005. "Contemporary Challenges to the Philosophy and Practice of Organization Development." In *Reinventing Organization Development: New Approaches to Change in Organizations*, ed. D.E. Bradford, pp. 19–42. New York, NY: Wiley.

Maslow, A. 1954. *Motivation and Personality*. New York, NY: Harper and Row.

McClelland, D. 1973. "Testing for Competence Rather than Intelligence." *American Psychologist*, 46.

McClelland, D. 1987. *Human Motivation*. New York, NY: Cambridge University Press.

McClelland, D., and Burnham, D. 2003. "Power is the Great Motivator." *Harvard Business Review*. http://hbr.org/2003/01/power-is-the-great-motivator/ar/1.

Mehrebian, A. 1981. *Silent Messages: Implicit Communication of Emotions and Attitudes*. Belmont, CA: Wadsworth.

Mintzberg, H. 1994. *The Rise and Fall of Strategic Planning*. New York, NY: The Free Press.

Mortensen, K. 2004. *Maximum Influence*. New York, NY: Amacom.

Nasi, J. 1994. In J. Nasi (ed.). *Arenas of Strategic Thinking*. Helsinki: Foundation for Economic Education.

"Is Neil Armstrong's Famous Moon-landing quote Really a misquote?" 2013. *NDTV:World.*http://www.ndtv.com/article/world/is-neil-armstrong-s-famous-moon-landing-quote-really-a-misquote-375900 (June 5).

Ohmae, K. 1982. *The Mind of the Strategist*. New York, NY: Penguin Books.

Patterson, A. 2009. "Creating a Talent Culture." *CMA Management*, pp. 11–13.

Patterson, K.E. 2012. *Crucial Conversations*. New York, NY: McGraw Hill.

Peters, T. 1982. *In search of Excellence*. New York, NY: Harper & Row.

Phillips, J. 1983. "Enhancing the Effectiveness of Organizational Change Management." *Human Resource Management* 22, no. 1–2, pp. 183–199.

Piaget, J. 1983. "Piaget's Theory." In *Handbook of Child Psychology* (4th ed., Vol. 1), ed. P. Mussen. New York, NY: Wiley.

Pink, D. 2005. *A Whole New Mind:Why Right-Brainers Will Rule the Future*. New York, NY: Riverhead Books.

Pink, D. 2009. *Drive*. New York, NY: Penguin Group.

Pink, D. 2012. *To Sell is Human*. New York, NY: Riverhead Books.

Porter, M. 1980. *Competitive Strategy: Techniques for Analyzing Industries and Competitors*. New York, NY: Free Press.

Porter, M. 1996. "What is Strategy?" *Harvard Business Review*. http://hbr.org/1996/11/what-is-strategy/ar/1

Robbins, S. 2011. *Organizational Behavior*. Upper Saddle River, NJ: Prentice Hall.

Sanders, T.I. 1998. *Strategies Thinking and the New Science*. New York, NY: The Free Press.

Smith, M. 2001. "Peter Senge and the Learning Organization." Infed. http://infed.org/mobi/peter-senge-and-the-learning-organization, (March 17, 2001).

Spencer, S.A. 1993. *Competence at Work: Models for Superior Performance*. New York, NY: John Wiley and Sons.

Spreier, S.E. 2006. "Leadership Run Amok." *Harvard Business Review*. http://hbr.org/2006/06/leadership-run-amok-the-destructive-potential-of-overachievers/ar/1

Tobin, D. 2012. "Not All Ladders Lead to Management." *Talent Management*. http://talentmgt.com/articles/not-all-ladders-lead-to-management, (April 20, 2014).

Uzzi, B.A. 2005. "How to Build your Network." *Harvard Business Review*. http://hbr.org/2005/12/how-to-build-your-network/ar/1

Vogelstein, F. 2013. "And Then Steve Said, 'Let There Be an iPhone.'" *The New York Times*. http://www.nytimes.com/2013/10/06/magazine/and-then-steve-said-let-there-be-an-iphone.html?_r=1& (October 6, 2013).

Wadsworth, B. 1984. *Piaget's Theory of Cognitive and Affective Development*. 3rd ed. London, UK: Longman Pearson.

Welch, J. 2005. *Winning*. New York, NY: HarperCollins.

Yankelovich. 1999. *The Magic of Dialogue*. New York, NY: Simon & Schuster.

Yukl, G. 2012. *Leadership in Organizations*. 8th ed. Upper Saddle River, NJ: Prentice Hall.

Zenger, J.A. 2002. *The Extraordinary Leader*. New York, NY: McGraw Hill.

Index

OTHER TITLES IN THE HUMAN RESOURCE MANAGEMENT AND ORGANIZATIONAL BEHAVIOR COLLECTION

Jean Phillips and Stan Gully, Rutgers University, Editors

- *Culturally Intelligent Leadership: Leading Through Intercultural Interactions* by Mai Moua
- *Letting People Go: The People-Centered Approach to Firing and Laying Off Employees* by Matt Shlosberg
- *The Five Golden Rules of Negotiation* by Philippe Korda
- *Cross-Cultural Management* by Veronica Velo
- *Conversations About Job Performance: A Communication Perspective on the Appraisal Process* by Michael E. Gordon and Vernon Miller
- *How to Coach Individuals, Teams, and Organizations to Master Transformational Change Surfing Tsunamis* by Stephen K. Hacker
- *Managing Employee Turnover: Dispelling Myths and Fostering Evidence-Based Retention Strategies* by David Allen and Phil Bryant
- *Effective Interviewing and Information Gathering: Proven Tactics to Improve Your Questioning Skills* by Thomas Diamante
- *Essential Concepts of Cross-Cultural Management: Building on What We All Share* by Lawrence Beer
- *Growing Your Business: Making Human Resources Work for You* by Robert Baron
- *Developing Employee Talent to Perform: People Power* by Kim Warren
- *Fostering Creativity in Self and the Organization: Your Professional Edge* by Eric W. Stein
- *Designing Creative High Power Teams and Organizations: Beyond Leadership* by Eric W. Stein
- *Creating a Pathway to Your Dream Career Your Dream Career: Designing and Controlling a Career Around Your Life Goals* by Tom Kucharvy

Announcing the Business Expert Press Digital Library

Concise E-books Business Students Need
for Classroom and Research

This book can also be purchased in an e-book collection by your library as
- a one-time purchase,
- that is owned forever,
- allows for simultaneous readers,
- has no restrictions on printing, and
- can be downloaded as PDFs from within the library community.

Our digital library collections are a great solution to beat the rising cost of textbooks. E-books can be loaded into their course management systems or onto students' e-book readers.

The **Business Expert Press** digital libraries are very affordable, with no obligation to buy in future years. For more information, please visit **www.businessexpertpress.com/librarians**. To set up a trial in the United States, please email **sales@businessexpertpress.com**.

CPSIA information can be obtained
at www.ICGtesting.com
Printed in the USA
FFOW05n0224181014

9 781606 499108